HIGHS in
THE LOW FIFTIES

how i stumbled through the
joys of single living

Marion Winik

Guilford, Connecticut
An imprint of Globe Pequot Press

for Beau

To buy books in quantity for corporate use
or incentives, call **(800) 962-0973**
or e-mail **premiums@GlobePequot.com.**

 skirt!® is an attitude . . . spirited, independent, outspoken, serious, playful and irreverent, sometimes controversial, always passionate.

skirt!® is an imprint of Globe Pequot Press

skirt!® is a registered trademark of Morris Publishing Group, LLC, and is used with express permission.

Text design: Sue Murray

Layout: Casey Shain

Library of Congress Cataloging-in-Publication Data
Winik, Marion.
  Highs in the low fifties : (how I stumbled through the joys of single living) / Marion Winik.
    pages cm
  ISBN 978-0-7627-8713-5
  1. Winik, Marion. 2. Authors, American—21st century—Biography. 3. Single women—United States—Humor. I. Title.
  PS3623.I66259Z46 2013
  818'.603—dc23
  [B]
                                                    2012050338

Printed in the United States of America
10 9 8 7 6 5 4 3 2 1

O gods! Who is't can say "I am at the worst"?
I am worse than e'er I was.
And worse I may be yet: the worst is not
So long as we can say "This is the worst."

The lamentable change is from the best;
The worst returns to laughter.

King Lear, Act IV
William Shakespeare

contents

prelude: things fall apart

1. the mattress professionals

One afternoon in the summer of 2008, a Sleepy's mattress truck driver turned down my driveway by mistake, then reversed and backed over my mailbox. Without a moment's pause, he zoomed off down the road. Surely this man had goods to deliver, a time clock to punch, beers to drink, bets to place, maybe someone waiting for him in a darkened room at the Rocky Ridge Motel, so hastily did he race away.

My estranged husband Crispin and I witnessed the felling of the mailbox through the windshield of my car while heading out of our once-shared driveway, a roller-coaster-like, quarter-mile-long lane on which we had squandered a small fortune for paving and plowing in our ten years together. We rural Central Pennsylvanians faced a preexisting mailbox problem, as smashing them with baseball bats from moving vehicles was one of the few interesting pastimes available to local youth. This made it all the more discouraging to see ours once again flattened, this time by someone who had better things to do. Now, rather than giving my ex a ride to pick up his car at the mechanic, I was involved in a high-speed car chase over the country roads of Glen Rock. We tailgated the Sleepy's truck furiously, honking and shouting at every stop sign, but the guy never even slowed down, rumbling past red barns full of staring cows like Steve McQueen in an eighteen-wheeler. At least it brought my ex and I together in an invigorating moment of shared outrage and vengefulness. At someone else.

It was up this very driveway our wedding guests had rolled in the magical May of 1999, back when gas cost less than a dollar, when the sky was blue, and the corn was high. They brought crawfish from New Orleans and hot sauce from Texas and tomato pie from Philly. They put on neon Afro wigs and sang and danced in the fields. They heard the bridal march played on accordion by the groom himself; they ate cream cake baked and brought in from the Poconos by my late first husband's mother. Many of them stayed at the Rocky Ridge Motel, which was in such poor repair that my childhood friend Carolyn Mahoney, now an interior decorator, had to go and buy new linens at Wal-Mart.

Crispin was a philosophy professor and a politics junkie, an op-ed columnist, a blues harmonica player, and a tattooed, pony-tailed nature boy. He was a bewitching combination of intense and laid-back, Redskins fan and intellectual, anarchist and libertarian. I went crazy for him after I met him in a bookstore in Maryland, and we had been long-distance lovers for over a year. We wrote impassioned letters, we wrote two million e-mails, we wrote poems and pornographic essays on nerve.com, we made up languages and countries. I lay in my bed in my underwear and read his published volumes of philosophy as if they were romance novels: *Obscenity Anarchy Reality* and *Act Like You Know.* As far as I could see, the whole point of the first forty years of our lives had been to bring us together, to merge our bodies and souls and vocabularies for all time.

When my boys and I moved from Texas to Glen Rock to live with him and the children of his first marriage (they visited each weekend), we obviously required something bigger than the little house he rented on an emu farm. I bought an imposing four-bedroom mansion on a hill that had just a few rustic drawbacks—a wood-burning furnace, a long, rugged driveway, no air-conditioning. It was a Georgian-style house, the young real estate agent explained, and they don't have air-conditioning in Georgia.

Ultimately, I planned to fix the driveway, replace the windows, put in central air and heat, and tack on a back deck—but first, I got pregnant and added a baby girl named Jane to the menagerie. I hadn't planned on more children, but now I was married to a man who liked kids so much he could have been a birthday-party entertainer. He even did magic tricks. He was certainly doing one on me: Abracadabra, a whole new life in a whole new world.

By the time the Sleepy's mattress truck rolled over our mailbox, my luck had changed. For one thing, the greatest love ever known had slid gradually and then more quickly into the biggest mess you ever saw. Pretty early on, the brilliant blue-eyed professor, who had deep, long-standing trust issues, had decided I was not to be trusted. In fact, during one of the many long, late-night phone calls we had in the early months of our relationship, he told me that he had a "black hole in his heart" from all the losses and betrayals he had endured. Did this discourage me? Oh, no. I was going to fix all that in a jiffy. A few months later, there was a brouhaha about my going to a matinee of *Shakespeare in Love* with a writer friend. Soon after, it turned out that my shirts were too low-cut. By then, I was so caught up in convincing him he was wrong about me that I would still be there doing it now if the situation hadn't been taken out of my hands.

Perhaps a wide-open extrovert who had made a career of publicly blabbing about every wild thing she'd ever done was not the most likely to succeed as the wife of a jealous man. Perhaps a girl who loves parties and restaurants should not marry a committed recluse. Perhaps an approval junkie should not pledge herself for life to a professional critic. But those are relatively good ideas compared to a union between a devoted drinker and a recovering alcoholic.

When I met Crispin he had been sober for nine years, and I thought that was very refreshing. I would quit drinking, too, just to be closer to him. Unfortunately, for the reasons suggested above, I gradually lost my enthusiasm for being quite so close to him, and I wanted a drink. So I had one.

A few years later, at a party in a palazzo in Italy where champagne flowed in icy rivers, he decided to join me.

When I saw him for the first time with a glass in his hand, I was horrified, assuming disaster was imminent. But for a while it seemed like everything was going to be fine. He was relaxed, gregarious, even flirtatious. There's a photo of him taken that night by one of his dance partners. He has a James Bond leer on his face and his bow tie is askew. Look, I exclaimed in delight when I saw it—it's next month's cover of *Relapse Monthly*. ALCOHOL SAVED MY MARRIAGE.

5

The next three years offered a strong counterargument to that proposition.

And, as it turned out, the collapse of the greatest love the world has ever known was just one part of the stinky package that would be stuffed in my mailbox before the man from Sleepy's put it out of its misery for good.

2. big jane

Moving from Texas to Pennsylvania to marry Crispin was a version of coming home for me, since I grew up outside Asbury Park, New Jersey, in the house where my mother, Big Jane, still lived. Now that I was back in the East and living three hours away, she could pop in anytime—pulling into our driveway in her silver SUV, honking for us to come out and help with her bags and golf clubs and coolers full of nova and shrimp, ready for a drink, a cigarette, and the ritual denunciation of the traffic on the Pennsylvania Turnpike.

In August of 2007, Big Jane felt a little strange on the last hole of the Better Ball tournament she had just won. She went into the hospital with breathing difficulties and was there for ten days. During this stay, they diagnosed her with lung cancer and put together plans for radiation and chemo. She had already survived two heart attacks,

a quadruple bypass, non-Hodgkin's lymphoma, and surgery on her digestive system. No doubt she would con-
quer this as well. We Winiks are a hardy people; we face
illness with disbelief, brute resistance, tenacity, and, if that
fails, in the words of my mother, "fucking disgust."

During the nine months of what turned out to be
our mother's final illness, my sister and I spent a great deal
of time in our childhood home, a fifty-year-old ranch
house at the Jersey shore. It was an hour and a half for
Nancy from Suffern, New York, and three hours for me
from Glen Rock, but we came as often as we could. It was
surely one of my mother's last pleasures—as golf, bridge,
theater, books, and even *Jeopardy!* were taken from her
(the theme song was playing on her TV at the moment
she died)—to see us mutate into The Winik Girls again.

As Nancy and I spelled each other at doctors'
appointments, in the hospital, and at her bedside, our
mother gradually turned over to us not just medical and
household decisions, but also the management of the
intricate, ruthlessly organized empire we referred to as
Jane Winik, Inc. My CPA sister was appointed treasurer,
and I became secretary. In general, and as always, both of
us were killing ourselves to please our mother, and we
mostly succeeded, but there were a few things she didn't
quite trust us on.

Even before the days of handing over safe-deposit keys and signing powers of attorney, my mother feared that my sister and I did not appreciate the value of the small number of artists' prints and oil paintings she and my late father had collected.

For one thing, she knew that this art was not to either of our tastes. There was the depressing Modernist cityscape, the twirling, impastoed tango dancers, the "cubist" snow-roofed barn, the obligatory Don Quixote in the powder room. But, she would point out, the Vasarely certainly is worth something! And the Calder!

My mother's Alexander Calder print, which hung in the living room under its own art lamp, was a large red, blue, and yellow abstract lithograph titled *Caracol,* No. 65 of 75, bought by my parents in 1980. On the day of the home sale we held to sell her remaining furniture and possessions (we'd already given thirty-seven bags of perfectly kept, size-six-petite suits, dresses, and golf attire to Jewish Child and Family Services), both it and the Vasarely were stowed in my old bedroom with other items not for sale.

The sale was to begin at 9:00 a.m. on a Saturday, and neither my sister nor I made it in time. When the real estate agent who was selling the house for us arrived at 8:30, there were already a dozen people waiting, and when he unlocked the door they streamed in. By the time

8

I arrived at 10:30, my sister was on the front lawn with one of my mother's best friends, discussing the theft of my grandmother's silver flatware. It had been in the drawer of a highboy, also not for sale. I went straight to the back bedroom and determined that the Calder was gone as well.

The rest of the day was a blur. The poor flummoxed real estate agent thought he might have sold a painting for $5 to a blonde lady who worked at Home Depot— he saw it only from the rear, while conducting another transaction. However, when we tracked her down, the blonde lady assured us that she had purchased the Toulouse-Lautrec knockoff, and that there was no Calder in the house by the time she got there. She surely would have known. Meanwhile, she asked, were we definitely not interested in selling the Vasarely?

By this time we felt we loved the obnoxious op-art Vasarely as much as anything we'd ever seen, and would no more part with it than we would our own children. As we discussed the mysterious thefts with the home-sale habitués who were present, we found ourselves deep into a sort of Agatha Christie-meets-Danny DeVito scenario. There were helpful neighbors picking through earrings, a ridiculously young cop scribbling on a notepad, a handsome junk dealer hauling out the living-room set. Everybody had a different opinion, another line of speculation.

Meanwhile, my mother's size-six-petite ghost seemed to float in the background, fingering the discolored rectangle on the wood paneling beneath the disconnected art lamp.

My mother had been dead six months and already so much had happened that she would have hated. Some of it was Wall Street's fault, some of it was the government's, but some of it, Nancy and I knew, was ours. Of course she would have forgiven us, but it's different when you have to imagine your own pardon.

My house is filled with my mother's things now: her bedroom set, her coffee cups, her bridge score pads, and her nail files. Each of these items sat in its own particular spot in that house on Dwight Drive for decades. What would my mother think if she could see them now in their strange diaspora, scattered around rooms she never saw in a city she never visited, a house where her cheesy tango dancers hang on a crimson wall and her Vasarely has a place of honor at the top of the stairs?

3. the rime of the ancient marion

Some of the bad things that happened to me in this awful period were completely my fault, results of my decaying mental state as an older single mom living in what had come to seem like a Georgian airplane hangar with my daughter and my dog. I had said good-bye to my husband and my mother, my boys had left for college, my step-children were gone, people were dying right and left . . . What else could I pitch into the trash?

Late that summer, Jane and I went to visit her best friend, Rachel Bacha, whose family had a summer place in Idaho. The mom, who had been having marital troubles as well, was a sturdy Glen Rock farm girl, easy on the nerves. A couple weeks in Elk City with her and the wildlife seemed like a good idea.

When Jane and I got to the Boise airport, I went to the Avis counter to pick up my rental car. I handed my Priceline.com confirmation to the agent. A perplexed look came over her face. "I'm sorry, Mrs. Winik," she said gravely, "this reservation was for June fifteenth." It was July.

Things went downhill from there as she explained that I had paid Priceline, not Avis, so only they could refund my money. Reached by phone, Priceline's representative said that while unused reservations could be refunded in certain circumstances, this one—the customer is a moron who doesn't know the difference between June and July—was not among them. She could only suggest that I go on their website and contact Customer Relations.

It was at this point I realized I had left my computer charger plugged into the wall in the gate at the Baltimore airport. Of course I had!

Now I had a whole new reason to live, a fresh impetus for placing desperate phone calls to persons unable to help me. Northwest Airlines. Airport Lost and Found. Basically, my life was now devoted to solving problems of my own creation.

Just a week earlier, I had spent the night in an airport hotel with my seventeen-year-old son Vince so he could make a 7:30 a.m. flight to Amsterdam. We stayed overnight in an airport hotel and got up at 4:30 that morning so we could be at the airport on time. But when Vince handed his e-ticket to the woman at the counter, she made the very face I would soon see on the Avis lady in Boise. The flight was 7:30 that evening. Vince would now have to spend fourteen hours in the Baltimore airport and had no way to get in touch with the friend who was meeting him in Europe. It was very nice of him not to just kill me right there.

If he had, at least he would have prevented the subsequent catastrophe.

Having totally screwed up Vince's departure to Europe, I moved on to fail his stepsister Emma, who needed to catch the Megabus to New York. This bus leaves from a Park 'n' Ride near the Ikea in White Marsh, a suburban outpost of Baltimore. Emma, Jane, and Beau, my beloved black-and-tan miniature dachshund, were in the car. We got there early, so hopped out of the car to wait and let Beau take a pee. We waited and waited, until it was obvious something was wrong. Turns out I had gotten confused about the time and had gotten us there twenty minutes late. The next bus wasn't until evening, so I decided to take the girls up to their dad's in Pennsylvania.

It wasn't until I had dropped them off and returned to my Georgian mansion that I realized the dog was not in the backseat. Nor was he at my ex-husband's when I called. Which meant we had left him at the Park 'n' Ride two hours earlier.

The sweetest, gentlest, most loyal and loving dog in the world, abandoned in a parking lot? With no tags or other identification? It was time to take me off life support. But first I had to call my twenty-year-old son Hayes, whose Christmas present Beau had been four years ago—a family joke, as I had repo'ed the dog almost immediately.

Hayes was interning at Merrill Lynch in Washington, D.C., and I reached him at his office. I was hysterical.

What Ikea was it? he asked.

The one in White Marsh, I screamed. In Maryland. We're never going to see him again!

Are you driving back down there? he asked. Just keep going. I'll make some calls.

A few minutes later, my resourceful young hero phoned to tell me he'd tracked down the dog at the security office at the White Marsh mall, across the street from the Park 'n' Ride. When I walked into that office, peered through the grate of the service window, and saw Beau lounging on a desk, my knees buckled and I went right to the floor. Beau poked his nose through the bars, stared at me for a moment, then started wagging his entire body.

Darn, said the woman who had just won the pool to take him home.

Everyone who heard these tales of woe was sympathetic. Many said they'd had similar problems. Some had left their kids in a parking lot. Others had ordered whole living room sets by accident. My condition was presumed to be aggravated by stress and bereavement, which can apparently drive you from fearsome competence to doddering idiocy, from being the efficient CEO of everyone's life to the retired boob in worn flip-flops, missing even her favorite TV show.

For some time after my mother died I could not successfully drive to even the most familiar destinations.

Lurching from a mental fog I hadn't even known I was in, I'd look around and have no idea where I was. Once I made a wrong turn in the endless fields outside Glen Rock on the way to a friend's house, and at least for a few minutes, was pretty sure I was lost for good. Or at least until Verizon fixed the gaps in its cell-service network.

When late that year, after months of dedicated badgering, I got a check for $100 from the Sleepy's mattress company for my mailbox, it seemed to mean I should keep trying and everything would eventually right itself. I just needed another whole new life in a whole new world. I had no idea where it was, what it would be like, or who would be in it, but I was on my way.

desperate housewives
of roland park

On February 1, 2009, I pulled up behind the moving truck in front of my new home, a sage-green row house on a tree-lined street in Baltimore. With me were the last two family members still in my charge, eight-year-old Jane and the dog. As the movers began to unload, I went in to make sure everything was clean and ready. It was, except the basement, where a crew of workers was still remodeling a rocky, inhospitable cave into a usable room. The contractor had explained that the job was bigger than he'd expected, and they'd probably be around for several weeks after I moved in. No big deal, I said. I didn't need the space until the boys came home to visit from college.

I stuck my head in the basement door to let the workers know I'd arrived. "*Buenos dias!*" I called.

Within the first few hours, one of my new neighbors had stopped by with a plate of chocolate chip cookies and her daughter Julianne, a fellow third grader at the school where Jane would start on Monday. When they left, they took Jane with them to their house. So I was alone in the kitchen, hanging pots on the rack over the stove, admiring a nice frying pan the previous owners had left behind, when an attractive, loose-limbed Latino man in a knit ski cap came upstairs to fill a bucket with water. The minute he saw me, his expression changed to a classic male moue of appreciation, the silent equivalent of a wolf whistle.

I stepped to the side to let him get to the sink and his paint-spattered plaid flannel shirt brushed my arm. Our eyes met. His were liquid black.

"*Gracias, señora*," he said when the bucket was full, and turned to go back downstairs.

"*Cómo te llamas?*" I asked.

"Humberto," he said, flashing me that look again before he shut the basement door. He had a way of gazing at me as if I were Aphrodite—as if my transcendent beauty demanded homage. If I had still been married to Crispin, I would have had to take a shower to get that look off me before he came home.

Sometime in the 1970s while driving from Florida to New Jersey, I exited I-95 in Baltimore. I was probably trying to avoid a toll, as I often was during this penurious phase of life. I spent the next several hours lost in a postindustrial wasteland, fringed with really bad neighborhoods, trying desperately to get back on the highway. This experience was the basis of my impression of Baltimore for decades.

The next time I came to Baltimore, it was 1998. I had been living in Austin, Texas, for twenty years; I was out on tour for my cheery book about being a widowed single mother. I met Crispin in the bookstore that night and moved across the country to marry him. Crispin lived halfway between Baltimore, the home of his ex-wife and kids, and Harrisburg, Pennsylvania, where he taught at a satellite school of Penn State. Get out a map and you'll see: It's Glen Rock, all right. On weekends, we met his ex-wife in a gas station in Hereford, the heart of Maryland horse country, to exchange the children.

The "ru-burbs," as I called my new locale—with its rural farms and suburban developments, its single Wal-Mart, many fast food outlets, and conservative Christian mentality—was never right for me. Once my marriage ended, it was sheer desperation.

I couldn't go back to Texas because I couldn't take Jane so far from her father, who had rented a house in the woods a couple miles away. It would have made sense to move to Baltimore, since I was already commuting to teach there, but at first I didn't even consider the possibility, probably because of my shattered mental state, described in the previous chapter.

Instead, I developed a deep irrational conviction that I had to live someplace with a view of the ocean. The closest thing I could find in driving distance was Havre de Grace, a Maryland town at the intersection of the Susquehanna River and the Chesapeake Bay. I had seen its lighthouse in the distance as I crossed the bridge; I imagined a quaint Breton village in France.

Without heaping unwarranted insults on Havre de Grace, this was incorrect.

Eventually a friend who had lived in Baltimore all her life slapped some sense into me. I had been thinking of the city as nothing more than a parking lot, she pointed out, but it was full of quirky delights I had yet to comprehend. She gave me the name of her real estate agent, a funny gay guy she was sure I would love.

Two weeks later, I shook hands with a tall, dark stranger in his real estate office. Ken Maher had sparkly brown eyes and a big Roman nose, and within moments we were telling each other the stories of our lives. Like me, Ken was floating around in the wreckage of the world he once knew: Within the space of few months, his brother had died, as had his adored grandmother, and his live-in boyfriend had been deported to Colombia. With no further ado, we grabbed onto each other's driftwood rafts, brand-new best friends.

About six months later, after patiently touring me through every neighborhood in town, Ken showed me a place in Roland Park, the area he'd been promoting from the start, since it had the only decent public elementary school in the city. Another excellent thing about this house was that it was around the corner from his. This was it.

On weekends, that very same Exxon in Hereford would be the spot where I met my former soul mate to hand off our daughter.

By the time Humberto was so jubilantly feasting his eyes on me, it had been over a year since Crispin and I had split up. The only man I'd been with in that time was . . . Crispin. But that phase was over; it had been six months since I had last driven like a zombie to his house after yoga class and thrown myself onto his bed, the vortex of sexual energy still swirling between us.

It had been half a year, but still I'd felt physically ill that morning when I realized there was a woman at his house. I had called at 8:00 a.m. with a frantic last-minute question about some stuff he'd left in the basement. When he didn't answer the phone, I called again. I called his landline and his cell about three times each, then texted and e-mailed. When he finally picked up at 10:30 and shouted, "What the hell do you want?" I absolutely knew.

Honestly I'd known since 8:01.

Have I mentioned the man's initials are tattooed on my shoulder? Rings were not enough for us, I guess. So when he came home on our first anniversary with an MW designed by his daughter Emma inscribed on his forearm, I rushed out to ante up.

My marriage could not have ended much worse than it did, and I'd been unhappy for years before we split. But somehow I was still profoundly entangled with Crispin emotionally, and I still had either nightmares or sex dreams about him every night. I might never get over it, it seemed.

Nonetheless, now that he was with someone else, that was that. I had to move on. But how? Go online? Hit the bars? Beg my friends to fix me up? Start cruising the Central Americans in the basement? Or somehow adjust to a life without passion?

Only the last of these was out of the question.

❧ ❧

Jane started school the Monday after we moved in, so I was alone in the house with the construction crew. Sitting at my desk grading papers, I was surprised when I felt someone standing behind me.

"*¿Qué haces?*" asked Humberto.

"*Trabajo,*" I replied. I speak very little Spanish, but I was able to explain that I am a writing teacher. And a writer. I gestured to my books, sitting on the shelf. Something about the way he looked at them suggested that it wasn't just that he didn't read English. It was that he didn't read.

"*¿Tu no lees?*"

He shrugged. "*No mucho.*"

I pulled down a book whose cover shows a picture of my first husband and me with our baby sons. He pointed to my name and tried to pronounce it. "Mah ree on . . . Weeneek. *¿Es tu?*"

"*Es la historia de mi primera . . . umm, mi primera . . .* marriage. *Mi esposo murió de SIDA.*"

His eyes widened. My first husband died of AIDS?

"*Hace mucho tiempo,*" I said. "Sixteen years."

He shook his head sympathetically and touched my cheek.

22

Most of our interactions lasted no longer than that. A couple of times a day, he found a reason to venture upstairs. If I was at the desk, he'd come up behind me and touch my shoulders or stroke my hair. If I was in the kitchen, he would just stand there and look at me.

One day, I decided to use Crispin's Amazon Prime account so I could get free shipping on some books I needed. This turned out to be the very last time I ever used it, because I saw that he had sent a copy of the Kama Sutra to his new girlfriend. I nearly passed out, even though I realized it was my own fault that I'd found this out, it was none of my business, and it was no surprise. I told myself to stop thinking immediately about whether this meant she was an innocent who needed to be initiated in the ways of the world or a super freak who would try things I never imagined.

But—did we ever even look at the Kama Sutra together? We did have a bunch of rubber electric dildos and stuff from when I did an article on sex-toy home parties for a women's magazine. I was thinking of the thing that looked like a cross between a jellyfish and a rubber tarantula and fighting tears when suddenly Humberto appeared behind me.

For the first time, I got up out of my chair and turned to face him. He put his arms around me and I leaned into his chest. He was muscular yet soft, much bigger than me where my husband was about my same size, and there was a sweet unselfconscious quality to the way he held his body, as if he'd never given much thought to his abs, his pecs, or his quads, which makes sense when you come from a place where hunger is the bigger physical fitness issue.

Our hug lasted a minute or so, then we pulled apart. "*Tu pelo*," I said, looking up at him, running my hand through his newly cropped hair.

"*¿No te gustas?*"

I smiled. "*Me gusta más largo.*" If this meant I like long hair, it was only sheer luck.

It went on like this for weeks—hugs, looks, confusing conversations—until I began to worry. By now all the other guys knew what was going on. Did they talk about us? Did he talk to them about me? What if they told the boss?

In fact, the other men were unfailingly nice to me, meticulously polite, and always helpful when I needed something. Every day, they all trooped upstairs and asked me if it would be okay to microwave their lunches, and we usually exchanged a few sentences about how great the basement was turning out. At some point, Humberto stopped going back down with them to eat. Instead, he sat at my kitchen counter and opened his plastic container of food and his bottle of orange soda.

"*¿Qué es eso?*" I wondered. It smelled so good. "*¿Tu cocinas?*"

No, he didn't cook it himself. He explained that the ladies on his street sold plate lunches to go for the workingmen. "*Ven aqui,*" he said, putting a forkful in my mouth.

"Mmmmm," I said as the masa melted on my tongue.

The next day, he brought me a foil package of fresh, hot tortillas.

When Jane got home from school, I rolled one up for her with butter and jam. "Humberto brought these for us," I told her gaily. "Isn't that so sweet?"

"Humberto?" she said, eyeing both me and the snack with suspicion in her big blue eyes. "Is he your boyfriend?"

"No, silly, of course not."

"Then why are you always talking about him?" she said.

Well, Miss Third Grader, good question.

At this point the crew was almost done in the basement and began alternating my project with other jobs. One day, Humberto pulled out his cell phone and asked me to put my number in it. I couldn't think why, since we could barely talk to each other, but I did it anyway. Sure enough, he called me often. He said *¡Hola!*, I said *¡Hola!*, then he would say something else which I had to ask to him to repeat two hundred times until we gave up. Then he said *Adios* and I said *Adios*.

Though we never kissed, unfortunate progress was eventually made on other fronts. He would run his hands over my body, but had a way of pinching whatever he got hold of that I couldn't stand. It wasn't your usual two-fingered pinch, but a whole-hand squeeze, as if he were juicing a particularly resistant citrus fruit. Finally I used Google Translate to look up "pinch."

"*No me pellizques*," I told him.

"*¿Pellizques?*"

"*Como eso.*" I did to him what he was doing to me.

He chuckled and pushed my hand away, but also looked a little hurt. No matter; I hadn't gotten anywhere, because the next time we were together he started doing it again. Had no woman ever told him about this problem before? No one would like this technique, I was sure. Didn't they complain?

The truth is, I liked it so little that I was beginning to cool toward him. Yes, he was cute, but the pinching delivered a message to me that nothing else had.

Really, we weren't right for each other.

But to put it in Pokémon terms, the ability of looking must be stronger than the ability of pinching, because looking beat pinching in this Poké-battle. When Humberto called a few days later to say he wanted to come over and see me, I didn't ignore it or pretend I didn't understand, as I had in the past. I made a plan. He would come on a Saturday, when Jane would be with her dad in Pennsylvania. I'd drive over to where he lived and pick him up around noon; except for the bus, he had no other way to get here.

It took about ten minutes for him to give me the directions, since he was saying *Fayette* but I was hearing *Fie-jet,* so didn't recognize the name of one of the biggest streets in town.

The day of our date, I was nervous. Why was I doing this, if I didn't really want to? I guess it seemed like my best chance—or even my only chance—to have sex, which I obviously had to do as a phase in my recovery. I put on black yoga pants and a stretchy, V-necked black shirt, and I drove across town to the barrio, where he was waiting for me, standing in the rain without an umbrella.

He was dressed up, sort of heartbreakingly, in an ironed shirt, pants of shiny, thin material, and black lace-up shoes. Though I liked him better in the hoodie and ski cap, I appreciated the sense of occasion. When we got to my house, I offered him something to eat. He didn't want food, but asked if I had any more champagne.

With my laptop open on the coffee table and Google Translate running harder than a shredder at Goldman Sachs, I was able to learn many new things about Humberto. Such as, he had three kids at home in El Salvador whom he hadn't seen for four years. And their mother— his wife? he was vague on this—had left him. (Actually, it looked to me like he had left her.)

The kids? Didn't he miss his kids?

Oh, yes, he did.

This is a sexy conversation, isn't it?

He was tossing the ball for Beau, which only showed how uncomfortable he was, since he usually treated the dog as some kind of large rodent. Despite the champagne, neither of us was the least bit bubbly as we trooped grimly upstairs to the bedroom.

He took off his shoes and lay on top of the quilt.

I took off my shirt—somebody had to do something, right?—but when he started some halfhearted pinching through my black bra, I rolled away.

Then he said, "*No tengo un condón. He olvidado.*"

He forgot his condoms? This seemed hard to believe, so we confirmed the translation. *Condón. Profilactico.*

Preservador. Perhaps I should try to tell him that my tubes were tied so we didn't need the *condón.*

"*¿Su marido murió de SIDA, no?*"

Oh, okay. AIDS. Right. I could have attempted to explain that I didn't have the HIV virus, but really, I just wanted to put my shirt back on. Meanwhile, he looked about to cry. "What's wrong?" I asked.

"*Estoy muy triste,*" he told me. "*Mi vida—es muy triste.*"

"*¿Por qué? ¿Cuál es el problema?*" I sat up and looked around for my discarded top.

"*Es mi hermano,*" he said, and the tears rolled. He told me that his brother was trying to come to the United States from Salvador and was stuck in Mexico. He needed money to pay the *coyote* or they would keep him there. It was very, very dangerous; when Humberto himself had come, he'd almost died. So, maybe, could I please give him some money? He looked at me with tortured hope, his dark eyes wet.

"How much money is it?" I wondered, my head poking through the stretchy black collar of my shirt.

He told me.

At this point, my eyes also filled with tears and I leapt off the bed. I mean, I felt bad about his brother, and I knew I wasn't Aphrodite, but this was pretty far to fall.

Before I took him home, we sat on my front porch with Google Translate and had as serious a conversation as we could manage. I tried to explain how I felt, and to reassure him that I knew how he must feel. I didn't think he meant to hurt me, but he had, and I didn't have three thousand dollars to spare. Also, I told him, you should never ask a woman for money in her bedroom. It just isn't done.

He may or may not have understood, he may or may not have cared, but it was time for me to drive him back to Fie-jet, where I would give him two twenties toward the cause. Then, if I knew what was good for me, I would close Google Translate forever and sign up for Match .com, where I might not find love but I would at least find people who were looking for it, perhaps ones in my age group who spoke English.

my first life

Many moons ago, when I was a wild, unhappy twenty-four-year-old graduate student with a job at Stanley Kaplan's SAT prep headquarters in Manhattan, some friends dragged me to Mardi Gras in New Orleans, which they envisioned as offering some sort of rest cure for my manic-depressive tendencies and my drug problem. There I met Tony Heubach, an irresistible, funny, elegant figure skater turned bartender whom I fell in love with at first sight, irrevocably and utterly. It made not the slightest dent in my enthusiasm that he was gay. It was certainly no secret, as he worked in a gay bar where most of the regulars were his ex-boyfriends, and that's where I hung out with him as the original rockslide of infatuation became a full-on avalanche.

Here is the two-minute version of why I married a gay man, in hopes that it may shed a few beams of light on the current narrative.

While this was not the first time I'd been crazy in love—I was a pony-league love-a-holic by the time I got out of fifth grade—before I met Tony, no one had ever matched me card for card. When our intensities collided, our trains jumped the rails. I don't think it meant that he wasn't gay, or even that he was truly bisexual. As far as I know, aside from a few unhappy experiences in his teens, he had never slept with another woman, or wanted to. I was an exception to his rule, which made the whole thing even more white-hot. Having a beautiful gay man change his life to be with me was like getting the Nobel Prize for lovability, and despite the sad outcome of this situation, I don't think I was ever quite as unhappy again.

There were many advantages to having a gay husband. He was fantastically neat and clean, and trained me in his orderly ways. He could cook, bartend, devise and execute wall treatments, garden, iron, arrange flowers, set a perfect table, and professionally cut and color my hair. He bought my clothes, he cleaned our pool, and he would eventually do the lion's share of child care. Still, the two of us settling down together was only a little like settling down, which was just right for two such unruly characters.

The year we got married, the first news reports about a mysterious virus affecting gay men, Haitians, and hemophiliacs were coming out. By then, Tony had become a hairdresser, I was writing computer manuals, and we had moved from our first apartment in the French Quarter to a house in Austin, Texas. Tony had dropped the last name of his homophobic father and become Tony Winik. I was sitting with the new Mr. Winik on the ledge of our pink-painted carport one afternoon when he said *Uh-oh,* and read me the article from the *New York Times.*

When we got tested, we learned that I was negative and he was positive. That was surprising, since our unsafe contact had included IV drug abuse. In any case, I wasn't that worried. I thought of AIDS as some silly little thing like Legionnaires' disease, which would be cured in a few weeks. I was ready to plump up the nest and start having kids. I had quit all my vices and read up on conception, and this bump in the road wasn't going to stop me. A child could only be infected with the virus by the mother through the blood in the placenta, so as long as I remained negative, our offspring would be in the clear.

I got pregnant easily, remained HIV-negative, had a fat and happy pregnancy. But the next spring, with the nursery painted, onesies stacked, car seat by the door, our baby was stillborn. No reason for this was ever found. Though I was counseled to wait at least six months,

Hayes was born less than a year after his brother died, and Vince was not far behind.

My impatience served me well for once, because our blissful days as new parents were short. By 1992, many of Tony's old friends from the French Quarter and some of our new crowd in Austin had fallen ill and died. Tony had been cutting hair at home and taking care of the boys while I continued working at the software company, but by then he was having physical symptoms as well as emotional ones. The latter involved visits to the Birmingham, Alabama, love shack of a louche architect named Tomé. Soon I had a big crush on someone else, too.

The last part of our eight-year marriage was a train wreck. It's little surprise that our sex life never really worked out; our second-biggest problem was that while I was a bubbling geyser of self-analytic conversation, Tony was inarticulate when it came to his feelings. Verbal attempts to solve our conflicts consisted of my stating my point of view, then my stating his point of view, then my offering the rebuttals for each side, while he rolled a joint, Windexed the French doors, and read the paper. And that was in the good times.

After about a year and a half of precipitous physical decline, Tony checked out of the Austin AIDS hospice on August 20, 1994, and came home to take a big handful of sleeping pills followed by a shot of Morton's No-Salt in the vein. I held a funeral on Mount Bonnell with a bunch of preschoolers releasing helium balloons.

I will spend the rest of my life missing him.

A couple years after Tony died, I went to Chicago to be on *The Oprah Winfrey Show* to promote the memoir I'd written about our marriage, the one I showed Humberto. At that time Oprah had not yet started her book club and was not known as a lover of literature, so I had my doubts about this outing from the start. When I heard her intro to the program ("TODAY WE MEET WOMEN WHO HAVE HAD THE EXPERIENCE EVERYONE DREADS—WHEN THEY HEAR THEIR HUSBANDS SAY THESE THREE WORDS: 'HONEY, I'M GAY!'"), whatever hope I had left—briefly fanned by the Best-Selling Author Barbie look created for me in hair and makeup—evaporated.

Most of the women on the show had discovered late in life that their husbands, clergymen and lawn-mower salesmen, were gay. Not me. As Oprah described my book, which she had clearly never read, it was "the strange life of a woman who actually *wanted* to marry a gay man" by the "NPR commentator Marion Nik." It was getting worse by the minute. She didn't even know my name.

"Why did you want to marry a gay man?" she asked with concern. "Did you ever have sex? Did your husband need to be really drunk to make love to you?"

"What?!?" I stammered.

She repeated the question, and I briefly thought of hitting her. Our one moment of connection occurred off-camera, when she took a close look at my periwinkle silk shantung Isaac Mizrahi blouse. Her face lit up and she asked me several enthusiastic questions about it.

By then I was dating an Irish food writer with a black leather jacket, a brushy mustache, and sea-green eyes. I'd fallen for him without much of break once Tony and I were through. He was the opposite of Tony in almost every way, and weighed twice as much as him. When the big man and I split up after five years, I fell right into Crispin's tattooed arms. Perhaps I was so unhappy in the pre-Tony years that I was afraid to be alone again. Certainly this was my state of mind when I arrived in Baltimore.

match dot bomb

Some people have good luck with Internet dating. Take
Crispin's fellow philosophy professor, Glen, a Woody
Allen type with a dangling ankh earring and the eyebrows of a cocker spaniel. He was the first person I ever
knew who went on Match.com, and he was engaged to
the girl he met there before the year was out.

My best friend Sandye also had a happy online love
story. Though she hadn't had a decent long-term boyfriend since the Carter administration, she had found Mr.
Wright—his real name—on Nerve.com. It only took a
few months, and there he was: intelligent, responsible,
good-looking, and fun, a sixtyish writer and editor with
a sexy Virginia accent. She lived in Brooklyn, he on the
northern tip of Manhattan; they might never have met
otherwise.

In Baltimore, my new friends Martha and Dan had
met on Match. Though Martha had been on the hunt

longer than Sandye, her process sounded efficient. She had a First Date outfit, a list of First Date restaurants, and clear criteria that determined the advance to Second Date and beyond. The system was obviously a success since it resulted in her meeting Dan, a kind, laid-back, and patient man. After several years, the two were now moving in together, along with the children of their first marriages.

There were others, of course—they were everywhere. I was introduced to a couple in Washington, D.C., who'd met on Salon.com when she was working as a wire-service reporter in Trinidad, he as a business consultant in LA. After two months of e-mails and phone calls, he flew four thousand miles for their first date. Not long after, they were married.

Surely it was time to start my free trial.

Meanwhile, there seemed to be other possibilities. Ken, the real estate agent who had found me my house in Baltimore and was now a good friend, had some ideas for me. He went over them one chilly night as he and Jane and I soaked in the disco hot tub in his backyard. Jane was having an easy transition from the farm to city living; she adored her school, and the cookie-bearing Julianne who lived down the block was her new best friend. Being able to walk everywhere—the school, the library, the bagel shop, the post office, Ken's hot tub—was very exciting for a little girl who had never gone on foot past her own mailbox.

As the underwater lights rotated from pink to green to blue, Ken enumerated the fellows he had in mind. One was a colleague in his real estate office, maybe a little old for me. Another was a guy named Jack he had known since childhood. Jack was super good-looking, he said, and really nice. Having recently broken up with his wife, he was having Ken take him around to look at bachelor pads. He probably wouldn't be available very long, I imagined, so I urged Ken to get to work.

Then we moved on to his love life, which had been rather depressing since his Colombian boyfriend José was deported a year before. I thought Ken should move on, but Jane, the nine-year-old romantic, favored long-distance love. She was also in favor of long-distance hate: Part of her enthusiasm for our life in Baltimore was the relief of its having ended the terrible situation between her father and me. Now I was calm and happy; he was sober and sane. The very few times she ever again heard us raise our voices to each other, she burst into panicky tears.

One weekend when Sandye was visiting from Brooklyn with her daughter Ava, we sent the girls overnight to Crispin's, and went out for a night on the town with one of my grad students, a party expert in thigh-high boots. I'd asked her to give us a tour of the places she would go to meet a man. We started at a little nook in her neighborhood. It was three deep at the bar, where I was quickly drawn into conversation by a paunchy, watery-eyed ex–Coast Guard captain.

After a while, Sandye touched my elbow. "Excuse me," she said to my dull new friend, "I need to borrow her." Sandye, it turned out, had been chatting with a guy who looked like a Calvin Klein underwear model, not the twenty-something kind but the seasoned thirties/forties type. He had forest-green eyes, white teeth, and sandy blond hair—if you'd seen him on Match.com, you would have been sure the person was using a fake picture.

Even more unbelievably, he turned out to be a molecular biologist working on a cure for cancer. This was one of the first things I learned when Sandye shoved me onto the stool beside him and left us to get to know each other. (Though his business card looked legitimate, I Googled him as soon as I got home. There I found his paper on highly specific cytotoxic effects on mammalian cells seen protease-resistant immunotoxins, which I planned to read just as soon as I had a minute.)

Nonetheless, there were drawbacks—or at this early phase in my dating career, I thought there were. The list was as follows: One, I didn't love his preppy look, a starched, blue-and-white pin-striped Ralph Lauren shirt tucked into blue jeans. Two, he talked a lot about how he loved living in the country and how he hated the city. (I was in the middle of the opposite conversion.) Three, he told me that he didn't get along with men because they are all such jerks; he only liked to hang out with women. Being the mother of sons, I argued this point. It seemed suspicious, anyway, to dislike one's whole gender.

Fortunately, there were a few positives to weigh against these turnoffs. For example, he was a dog person, and was clearly crazy about his teenage daughter. He was intelligent, well-spoken, and, as noted, super-cute. Young, but maybe not too young, because at least at that moment, he seemed very interested in me.

In the glow of his close attention, I told him a lot about myself. I described my books, my marriages, my children, my job. I told him I was thinking of going online to find dates, and asked him if he knew about that. A little, he said.

I asked if he thought I should lie about my age, since I didn't know if most men would include women of fifty in their search criteria.

"You should never lie about anything," he told me.

Soon our blue-jeaned knees were touching, as were our elbows on the bar, and then all of a sudden he leaned over and started kissing me. And I kissed back.

Then, just as suddenly, it was too much. Too fast, too weird a setting, too important a thing to be happening in these circumstances. I pulled away, leapt up from the stool, and said, "Sorry—I have to go."

"Really?" he said. "Where are you going?"

"Well . . . we were going to go dancing," I said uncertainly, then with more conviction. "At that bar on the top floor of the Belvedere Hotel. You could come with us. . . ."

"Oh, I'm not much of a dancer," he said. "Why don't you and your friends go have fun. I'm about to head home anyway."

"Okay, if you're sure," I said. "We'll e-mail. Right?"

"Yes," he said. "Don't worry. I understand."

I kissed him once more, lightly, on his scratchy, clean-smelling cheek.

"What happened?" the girls wanted to know when we got out on the sidewalk. "Are you crazy or what?"

"I don't know! I guess—well, it was my first kiss, and it just scared me all of a sudden. It didn't feel right."

"What's your problem, exactly?" Sandye asked. "Is it that he speaks English? That he bought you a drink? Maybe we can find you a homeless guy out here on the street."

Over the next couple of days I kept looking at the business card on my desk and wondering if I should write to Mr. Underwear Model Biologist, and if so, what I should say. Sunday morning, he beat me to it. "Sorry if I was a little forward with you," he wrote. "I don't get out very often."

This e-mail kicked in a delayed response to his charms. I wrote a long reply, describing the rest of our night on the town and apologizing for my behavior. However, after that he was always busy—getting lattes, going to the gym, doing things with his daughter, curing cancer. The next and only other time I saw his face, it was on Match.com. The time had come; I had put up my profile.

My profile was fine-tuned with the help of Sandye and Mr. Wright, Martha and Dan, and the Underwear Model Biologist himself, who had morphed from prospect to mentor. He helped me choose my pictures, hone my headline, and explained that not answering certain questions was not the same as lying. It was probably better than scaring people off with visions of an atheist chain smoker with a houseful of runny-nosed brats.

As soon as I posted my profile, I started hearing from prospective suitors. Some wanted to "challange" me to a game of "Scrable." Others were more romantic: "marion,

TripleEarth
Sassy, sensual, and smart.
50-year-old woman
Baltimore, Maryland, United States
seeking men 40–57

Relationships:	Divorced
Have kids:	No answer
Want kids:	No answer
Ethnicity:	Caucasian
Body type:	Slender
Height:	5'4" (163 cms)
Religion:	No answer
Smoke:	No answer
Drink:	Social drinker

for fun:
I love to eat, drink, and be merry. Talk, walk, and play Scrabble.
Dance. Go to the beach. Go out to dinner. Laugh. Make you laugh.
Listen. Tell stories. Hear stories. Go to the movies. Have adventures.
Travel. Kiss.

my job:
I'm an author and I teach creative writing to grad students. I have an
advice column in a women's magazine.

my education:
BA, Brown University, 1978; MFA, Brooklyn College, 1983.

favorite hot spots:
Austin, New Orleans, Mexico, France, Montreal, the Caribbean, and
my hometown of Asbury Park, New Jersey.

favorite things:
I love books and talking about books. I love Prince, Neil Young, the Talking Heads, the Dead, Lou Reed. I don't watch TV much but can get into a football game. Breakfast tacos. Cocktails. Not together. Usually.

last read:
Philip Roth, Grace Paley, Lorrie Moore, Tony Hoagland, Michael Chabon, J. D. Salinger, Garcia Marquez, Junot Diaz, Dave Eggers. Also the Sunday *Times* and *The New Yorker*.

my pets:
I am a dog lover.

about my life and what I'm looking for:
I'm a very real, very open person with energy and passion to spare. I love to laugh, and I can see the lighter side of almost any situation—an ability I've had plenty of chances to hone over the years. A super-loyal friend and companion, I still am very connected to many of those I've crossed paths with in this life. My sons are in college and my ex has our daughter on weekends, so I have some time on my hands. I need someone to show me my new neighborhood.

about me:

Hair:	Dark brown
Eyes:	Blue
Exercise:	Exercise 3 to 4 times per week
Politics:	Very Liberal
Sign:	Taurus
Pets I have:	Dogs
Pets I like:	Birds, cats, exotic pets, fish, horses, other

I am going to be up front with you. I want to become your man in life. I am not kidding. So what do i have to do to date you and start hangout with you for fun. so please talk to me marion. I could be yours."

Unfortunately, the forty- to fifty-seven-year-old age group seemed to be full of seventy-year-olds. Hair was rare. Guts were expansive. Complexions were pasty or suspiciously rosy, and spelling was surely a lost art. I learned to scout the background of the self-taken cell-phone photographs for the rigging: In Baltimore, the sailboat is everything.

Even after ruling out the grammar abusers and other nonstarters, including the three people on Earth who don't enjoy walking on the beach, I found myself skittish. Just being over fifty seemed to have reduced the pool to a puddle, and a scary part of it was composed of twenty-one-year-old perverts. The screen names alone—Passion4U and SuperGrande and BBQRavensMan—scared me off. I was easily spooked by phrases like "Christian/Catholic," and "I'll tell you later."

But people were skittish about me, too. Several times, after I'd told a man I was a writer and he'd looked at my website and read my life story, he would stop writing to me altogether. It might have been my résumé. It might have been AIDS or atheism or Jane. Still, I found myself unable to withhold the information. I was already such a public person that withholding details seemed coy. I couldn't grasp the fine line between advertising and self-exposure.

The first man I made a date to meet had many good points. He was not only an excellent speller, he was a doctor. He had graduated from Brown the year before I got there. He was a dog lover who lived just a few blocks away. Before we met in person, he wiped the floor with me in a game of online Scrabble, playing words like HM and FEAL (both legit, as it turned out). It was hard to set up a meeting due to his professional responsibilities, golf games, and stringent TV-watching schedule, but we did finally manage to schedule an 8:00 a.m. breakfast before his Sunday tee time, at a restaurant down the block.

My pal Martha chose my outfit for the occasion— actually, Martha supplied the outfit, since she had all that retired First Date wear. She gave me a pair of hip-huggers, a wide leather belt, and a soft, heather cashmere sweater. Dressed as Martha, I strolled into Miss Shirley's and found the man I'll call Uncle Norm.

Though Uncle Norm was only six years older than me, my first impression was that he was from a different generation. He reminded me so much of my parents' friends, the funny, amiable Jewish golfers I had grown up with—i.e., old people—that I panicked immediately at the thought of us as a couple. Within moments of sitting down I had enthusiastically blurted, "Oh, we can be friends!"

Uncle Norm looked taken aback. "Well," he said, "I guess that's a pretty clear reaction."

We managed to have a nice breakfast anyway, but our relationship devolved immediately into phone calls, e-mails, and online Scrabble games. Soon we dropped the calls and notes and just sent Scrabble moves back and forth. Then I invited him over one night to watch *American Idol* with Jane, Ken, and me. That worked well for everyone, and we settled into a spot on his TV-watching roster that we have occupied ever since. He would bring with him his cute little black-and-white dog, who was so smart he got you a tissue when you sneezed, and a Styrofoam box of healthy Asian takeout. He would usually come barging in after the show had started, still talking to a patient on his cell phone. After a while, he was talking to his new girlfriend, a yoga teacher from D.C. he had met on Match.com.

Uncle Norm disappeared from our lives completely when the *American Idol* season ended, but has faithfully returned each season since. "Uncle Norm!" shout Jane and Ken and I in unison when he suddenly appears with his takeout and a big pack of Twizzlers during the season opener.

It doesn't sound so terrible now, but this first Match date shook me up. I hated walking into that restaurant, having a negative reaction, and feeling compelled to let the other person know. Moreover, I did a lousy job of it. And though Uncle Norm actually was friend material, I could see myself ending up with quite a number of unneeded new friends, dragging behind me like tin cans on a wedding car, except without the wedding or the car.

What I didn't yet realize is that something even less pleasant could happen.

Jane and I were visiting Sandye and Mr. Wright at her place in Brooklyn one night. We were sitting around drinking bourbon and talking about my troubles after the kids had gone to bed. I told them there was no one online in Baltimore—no one. They felt I was being too picky. So I logged them into my Match account and they did some searches for me. They were too un-picky, I thought, showing me all kinds of drab-looking weirdos, where I was screening for someone more like Brad Pitt.

Squinty eyes, low-hanging ball caps, dramatic overbites and underbites: None of this bothered them.

"This dude sounds like fun," Mr. Wright said, and read aloud. "I am a Tall, Outgoing, Athletic, 'Down-To-Earth' Guy who would like to meet an Attractive 'Down-To-Earth' woman who has some similar interests as mine and enjoys making the most out of every day. I love to Travel (All 50 States, 48 National Parks, and 91 Countries so far), Road Trips, Playing All Sports! (GO Ravens/Orioles /Terps! I am Originally from Baltimore!)"

I looked over his shoulder. It was a photo of the young Matthew Broderick, I believe. Unfortunately, the capitalization and use of quotation marks alone made this candidate out of the question for me. Reading online profiles was a very unfortunate way for a writing teacher to get to know people. It was much better if they turned up plastering her basement.

"Okay, what about this Bmoreguy?" said Sandye. "He's cute, he can spell, and he has a job!"

Hmmmm. Yes. Bmoreguy had decent pictures, including one of him jumping off a cliff into a lake that I liked a lot. His profile was literate and funny, including dialogue and sly humor. I shot him a message, he wrote back, and we eventually set up a time to meet for bagels at a corner cafe in my neighborhood. From the outset, he didn't seem quite as enthusiastic as I was, but perhaps it was just his style.

In person, Bmoreguy resembled his pictures, which was a good start. He had brown hair and blue eyes. He wore glasses, a tweed blazer, and jeans. He was a nice size—maybe five-foot-ten, with a little extra around the middle. Not full-on teddy bear, but teddy bear lite. He talked mostly about his daughters, his big, alcoholic Irish family of origin, and his social activism, which had turned from a hobby into a full-time job, though his other career was investing. I was intrigued by that paradox. He was extremely opinionated, and hated many things most other people in town love, like the television show *The Wire*. According to him, it was a derivative commercial rip-off of a genuine Baltimore identity. I was interested in all this passion, although sneering and disdain were specialties of my ex-husband and still made me nervous.

Since we were so close to my house, I suggested he walk me home. Then he came in. My son and his girlfriend were in the kitchen making a late breakfast. Hayes, now a junior at Georgetown, was on his way to an internship at Goldman Sachs that summer, and Bmoreguy gave him some thoughts and encouragement on that topic. He seemed completely relaxed in my house, petted my dog, and kissed me on the lips on the way out the door. I felt a little tingle.

I didn't hear another word from him for a week. I knew he was going on a road trip with his daughters, but I also knew there were Internet connections in South Carolina. Uncoolly, I wrote several messages without hearing back, and about ten days out, I wrote the uncoolest message of all. "Is just disappearing the usual way of saying 'I don't think so' in these parts? I thought I felt a little click there, but perhaps it was just the result of your having good 'people skills.'"

Uncool, but it got me an answer. He agreed that I was probably just confused by his excellent people skills. "You are a very interesting woman," he wrote, "but I didn't respond to you carnally."

My feelings were badly wounded by this—*carnally*, I kept saying to myself, feeling like a crossed-off sexless old crone, but also thinking of meat and flowers and the old movie with Ann-Margret and Art Garfunkel.

I couldn't believe I had given a total stranger a free ticket to do this to me. I decided I was finished with Match.com. One way or the other, it was just a machine for rejection. They smacked you or you smacked them; either way it sucked. Meeting people in real life might be difficult, but it seemed much less risky.

However, I still had a few days on my one-month membership, and my thriftiness got the better of me. Jane was very interested in helping me look, but she wasn't much better at finding gold among the geeks and grandpas than I was. I think it was hard for her to believe that people this old even had love lives. (Can you imagine helping your mother shop online for a boyfriend? What the hell is this world coming to?) Finally, an eleventh-hour search turned up an attractive screenwriter named Dogsong. Though he was ten years younger than I, everything he said he wanted in a girl was . . . me. I wrote a clever e-mail about singing dogs, urging him to check out my profile and see how perfect I was for him.

"Thanks, but I don't think so" was all he wrote in reply.

Oh! That wasn't good. But to make sure he was really rejecting me—me?? Really??—I wrote again. "Are you sure? Aren't you blowing me off kind of quick?"

"No, I am not interested, and if you are so thin-skinned, you shouldn't be on Match.com," he replied.

Almost in tears, I had to admit that "thin-skinned" was right. One month on Match and I was practically cellophane. Any free-range Internet dickhead who took it into his head had the power to make me feel worthless. No more Dogsong for me. I went to a Leonard Cohen concert with one of my girlfriends and cried my eyes out on every song. "I'm your man," he sang, and I sobbed so loudly that people in surrounding rows began to give me the evil eye.

By now my thirty days were up, anyway, and I turned my sights to the real world. At a party at work, I met an impoverished, unsuccessful musician with a shock of white hair and black Johnny Cash clothes. The poor man had a rough audition when he came out for a burger with me, my three kids, and Ken one afternoon—admittedly, an unusual first date. For one thing, he was extremely worried about being followed, watched, robbed, or written up in the tabloids. His address was a secret, and he did not use his real name. But other than the fact that he lived in a really bad neighborhood, we could see no reason for his paranoia. Hayes and Vince, who were home for spring break, forbade me to ever see him again, not least because their sensibilities were deeply offended by his see-through vinyl backpack. Furthermore, when I walked him to the car, he told me he had a live-in girlfriend with a shotgun.

Meanwhile, Ken still hadn't gotten me a date—the realtor was all wrong, he'd decided, and Jack, the newly divorced hottie, was already seeing someone. Damn, Ken! To make it up to me, he took me out to Jay's on Read, a gay piano bar I love. Honestly, I love all gay piano bars. At this one, the piano player looks remarkably like Bill Murray, and he does songs like "I Say a Little Prayer for You," "I Feel Pretty," and "New York, New York." I sing my heart out, and all the old gay guys there love me much more than anyone on Match ever did, or will.

the summer of our discontent

I turned fifty-one, Jane turned nine, and our first summer in Baltimore began. I didn't see any romantic prospects at the swimming pool, the wine bar, or in the parking lot outside Jane's theater camp. Maybe I needed to look farther afield. One June weekend Jane, Beau, and I drove up to Woodstock, New York, to visit our hilarious friend, journalist and memoirist Martha Frankel, and her husband, visionary artist and vintage car buff Steve Heller.

Alas, even Martha (who knows everyone, including Robert De Niro, Jane Smiley, and God) and Steve (who has built a life-size *Tyrannosaurus rex* out of rusted spare parts) couldn't think of anyone for me. But while I was up there, we went out to visit my old summer camp, and this mission led to a confusing non-situation which took up most of the summer. When it was over, I had two new brassieres, a pair of lacy black underpants, and the remnants of some pretty sky-blue nail polish on my toes, none of which had even been given a test drive. Beau was the true beneficiary, having been switched to a more natural, delicious, and expensive brand of dog food and a more humane style of leash as a result of this odd liaison.

As children, every summer my sister Nancy and I were shipped off for a month to some nightmarish hellhole with no indoor plumbing; our bitter complaints never convinced my mother to let us stay home, but we did manage to get switched to a different camp every year. Eventually, she thought, one of them would be right.

Amazingly, one was. It was a camp I found in the classified section in the back of the *New York Times* magazine. In contrast to the other camp ads, which contained black-and-white photos of leaping youths and dreaded terms like *archery*, this one was two simple lines of sans serif type in a small white box, followed by an address.

for young people
interested in doing things

Camp Greenfields, as it was called, was located on a beautiful piece of land just outside Woodstock, New

York—the town's name alone was magic. It took ten boys and ten girls between the ages of twelve and sixteen, and we lived in long, bungalow-style dormitories with flush toilets and hot showers—a spa compared to the other camps I had seen. No sports of any kind were required except hiking and Frisbee; our days were spent taking classes from local craftspeople in stained glass, copper enameling, and jewelry making. At night, there were outings to the theater and rock concerts. We had definitely found our place in the world of sleep-away camps, and both of us attended for several years, around which time the camp closed anyway. It was really just too good to last.

Rudy Hopkins—the man who ran this place for those five years in the early seventies, who shepherded us through our Boone's Farm and marijuana experimentation, our teenage melodramas, and our training in cooking, cleaning, and other "community service" activities, who dragged us up the side of Slide Mountain and into Devil's Kitchen and off the edge of the Spillway—was still there on the property when I showed up that weekend, now operating a craft gallery out of the various buildings. In the thirty-five years since I'd seen him, his wild curly hair had grayed and his face had creased and weathered, but his leonine demeanor had lost none of its roar.

"How is your head?" were the first words out of his mouth once we had confirmed that yes, it was me coming up the walk. He was referring not to the contents of my skull, but to my scalp, which had suffered an injury my last summer there that had apparently been as unforgettable to him as it was to me. Bent over a bracelet I was working on with a silver-polishing tool running in my hand, I had thoughtlessly reached up to brush back my hair and the spinning shaft had wound my long locks round and round, tighter and tighter, right off my head. Our instructor had just warned loudly against this exact maneuver, I was later told. I was half-bald for many months (one of two times in my life, actually; a few years later I would have a very unfortunate permanent wave immediately before leaving the country and spend three months in East Germany with no hair . . . a story for another time, children).

I was so happy to be reunited with Rudy, and to show him my hair, and to find the place filled with as many utopian vibrations and floating lily pads as ever. After a few glasses of mint lemonade followed by a few glasses of white wine, we decided that I would try to organize a Greenfields reunion. It might be difficult to find some of the old campers—at this point, Rudy had no more than a few e-mail addresses—so we decided to delay until the following summer, giving us more than a year to track people down.

There were two former Greenfielders that Rudy had seen recently and would be easy for me to connect with, as they lived in New York City: Peter and Arnie. Peter, whom I had always adored, was the cool and witty son of a well-known poet. Back then, he was a heartthrob with dark eyes and luxuriant masses of dark-brown hair. Now he was bald and gay, but as delightful as ever when I met him for dinner in Brooklyn. He came over to Sandye's and made excellent margaritas and we planned to create a Facebook page to gather our old compadres.

If I had not already been married to a gay guy once before . . . if Peter didn't already have a boyfriend . . . if he hadn't already broken my heart once by going off with Tina Somebody that night on Slide Mountain . . . ah, well, it was not to be.

Arnie, the other camper Rudy had recently seen, I remembered as a grumpy little fellow, but Rudy said he was now a noted art photographer, and very sweet. He came to dinner later that summer, when I was back in Brooklyn visiting Sandye and my stepdaughter, Emma.

Emma is the older of Crispin's two children; like Hayes, she was then a senior in college. She was finishing up at the Gallatin School at NYU in a major of her own design, "The Aesthetics of Healing." She is an adorable, brown-eyed super genius, and we had become instant best friends when I'd met her dad ten years earlier.

Though our connection had undergone a little wear and tear during the dark days of the breakup, we still got along fine and spoke openly about our feelings.

By this time, I had become very anxious about my tattoo of her father's initials, which I'd gotten shortly after he'd shown up with his. Unlike him, I had failed to enlist Emma's design assistance, and while his tattoo seemed pleasingly artistic and vague, mine was nothing but a big old CGS. Indeed, that was what I'd wanted at the time. Now, even in a sleeveless shirt I felt uncomfortable, branded with the logo of the wrong owner. If I ever got another boyfriend, or even had sex again, it would be really weird. Doggie-style was out for good. Since laser removal was expensive and would leave a scar, I was now contemplating whether it could be made into something else without covering my whole back with some unwanted image. I had gone into a tattoo shop where I was shown perplexing photographs of how a graveyard scene could be turned into a Tasmanian devil, or a naked girl into the Grim Reaper.

One night Emma stopped by Sandye's. She and Jane went to work on the situation with a Sharpie.

"It's a snake!" Jane said. "Don't you like it?"

"It's very creative," I said, as I studied the photo on my iPhone screen. "A snake. Hmmmm."

Not long afterwards, there was a knock at the door.

"Hello! Is this the Greenfields camper meet and greet?" Arnie asked when I opened Sandye's door and found him standing there with his dog. He was a tall, pleasant-looking guy with the dark brown eyes I remembered, though the dark brown curls were now close-cropped and graying. Weirdly, he seemed to be doing a Pee-Wee Herman imitation.

"Hey, Arnie," I said. "What's your dog's name?"

"Oh, this isn't my dog," he said. "I found him on the way over. Would your friend be able to keep him?" Of course it was his dog, named Platypus as it turned out. Welcome to Arnie World. Something about his demeanor led me to wonder if he, too, had turned out gay.

Another night, after a dinner of take-out falafel, the whole gang of us walked over to Prospect Park for an outdoor concert: Sandye and Mr. Wright, Jane and Ava, me and Arnie, catching up on our lives and loves. Actually, it was more like getting to know one another in the first place, since we didn't remember each other well from Greenfields. Later, I took his arm on the walk back from the park. It was a nice feeling, and he kissed me lightly on the lips when he said good-bye.

Was there any click between us? I had a conceptual problem that was impeding my thought processes in this area. Given the way things had gone in my life up to that point, I had the impression that when one thing ends, you just turn around and the next is right there. Whatever man happened to be standing in my immediate line of vision was obviously being proposed by destiny as The One. All righty, then! Rush out, get a pedicure, fall in love.

So . . . we were both in the arts, right? And dog lovers. He was easy to talk to, nice-looking, and every once in a while, one of his jokes was funny. He had confided toward the end of the evening that he had a lot of mood problems and was taking antidepressants. That was the clincher. I love depressed people. I invited him down to Baltimore to visit sometime. A few weeks later, he e-mailed me to say that he and Platypus were coming for a week in July.

Again with the preparations! I went out and rented a DVD of season one of *The Wire*, with which he was obsessed. I stocked up on beer and planned meals from every corner of the world. I cleaned my house. Not knowing which way things would go, I bought both pretty new underwear and a quilt for the guest room.

The day of his arrival, he was supposed to get in at 12:30 p.m. I was up at 5:00 a.m. I had my crab cakes ready to go in the oven, a casual yet slinky outfit selected, my toenails painted sky blue. Then he called at 12:45 to say he was stopping at a flea market in Towson on the way into town.

I wasn't happy to hear this, as he had already asked if we could go to a flea market and I'd said no. It didn't fit into my plans for the day, and anyway, I hate flea markets. I guess he must have gone and Googled the matter himself.

I drove out to meet him and spent the next hour managing Platypus, who took a giant dump right in the middle of one of the aisles, while Arnie meticulously scrutinized each table of wares and asked questions like "Do you think this ashtray has the original finish?"

Finally we got home and ate crab cakes while watching an episode of *The Wire*. "Will we be able to go on a *Wire* tour?" Arnie asked. He had heard there was a driving route you could take to see all the famous landmarks of the television show. Unfortunately, it was also the driving route for buying crack, getting carjacked, and being the victim of a drive-by shooting.

Anyway, we never could have fit it in between the used bookshops, antiques stores, and other shopping packed into the days ahead. I watched him paw through piles of dusty merchandise in every such place in Baltimore, where there are many such places, me gritting my teeth all the while. We also took Jane to the swimming pool a couple of times, providing me with the slight thrill of having neighbors wonder why I was suddenly appearing with a male companion. I don't think it ever even occurred to Jane that he was supposed to be a romantic prospect; she assumed that we were some kind of vague old friends or distant cousins. Others, however, were more hopeful.

"Who's *that?*" Barbara Jones finally came out and asked. "A new boyfriend?"

"Beats me," I said.

It didn't seem like it, honestly. I would sit next to him on the couch while we watched *The Wire* and he wouldn't put his arm around me or anything, even if I tentatively touched his hand. Then one night after we'd had a little party at the house, I went into the guest room and lay down on the bed to chat. That led nowhere, so I eventually clumped down the hall to my own quarters.

The sensual peak of the whole experience was when we went to hot yoga class together. Arnie was surprisingly good at yoga, very flexible and graceful for a man. I looked over at him during Savasana—so relaxed and restful, so male. His eyelashes were very black against his cheek. I felt for a moment that I might be attracted to him.

Chaste as it was, I did like having a man around. I liked cooking and fussing over him, waiting on him and making my elaborate ethnic meals. I learned his routines: He drank his coffee cold, in the blender with ice. He put salt on everything. Every day he glugged down some weird concoction he'd brought with him, a smelly, raw vegetable puree with mystical nutritive qualities. He was a man of definite ideas and tastes, and not particularly open to persuasion. A testy man, a bossy man, a man who enjoyed anger and vendettas and diatribes, a man who often yelled at people on his cell phone for hours, and could get very annoyed by Facebook.

When he left it was confusing. Absolutely nothing romantic had happened—all the cute underwear still had the tags on it—and clearly nothing was going to happen. Jane could have told me this, and yet, I thought it my duty not to give up altogether.

The next time I saw him, it was in New Jersey. He came to visit at Sandye's mother's house, down the street from where I grew up. There, he spent most of the day gardening and flirting with Sandye's seventy-something mother. I think he may have invited her to Paris. Then that night he and I took the dogs down to the beach. There was plenty of moonlight on the onyx waves and the silvery sand, so I climbed up on the high lifeguard bench and waited. He did not climb up after me, busy as he was roaming the beach with his camera, attempting to photograph sand crabs. At this point, I became a little testy myself.

Since there really was nothing to change about our relationship—it already was a friendship—it was just a matter of resetting the tone of things, kind of like changing the wallpaper on your computer desktop from a bouquet of red roses to a sand crab.

Arnie and I had been talking about going on a road trip together to visit Rudy up in New York State. After the New Jersey experience, I e-mailed him to say that given my new understanding of our relationship, we should not go on this trip. Instead he should go to Paris with Sandye's mother.

This was the first time there had been any mention of our "relationship," and his response was obviously designed to spare my ego. "I am at a stage in my life," he wrote, "where I kind of want to get married and, if possible, have offspring. Plus, I am too messed up to be with someone now; I need to be alone to work out my issues. I wouldn't want anything to happen between us that would ruin our friendship in the long run."

I sent him a nice e. e. cummings poem—*since feeling is first who pays any attention to the syntax of things*—for his troubles, and we did remain friends. He continued e-mailing me his photographs of fossilized bird skeletons, Amazonian insect life, and Russian blast furnaces. I've been to several of his art shows—totaling my car on the New Jersey Turnpike on the way to one of them—and then we both went to the Greenfields reunion last summer, which was really fun even though there were only six people there. Platypus barked all night, and Jane and I didn't get a wink of sleep in our tent. It was perfectly fine.

Once our non-relationship was over, Arnie was very supportive of my dating career, and once even tried to fix me up with someone. Unfortunately it was the night of that bad car accident, and the guy didn't even notice the big, fresh purple bruise below my collarbone. He launched straight into a disquisition on the "lucid dreams" he has that allow him to see into the afterlife. Honestly, I didn't want to hear about it. Once he did finally catch on to my situation, he informed me earnestly that we have accidents when we need to release stress in our lives.

When he e-mailed me the next day to see if we could get together, it turned out that I did know how to say no, after all.

dreamboat

Given my romantic proclivities and history, not to mention the emotional beating I had taken in the past couple of years, perhaps better than "Sensual, sassy, and smart" for my dating profile headline would have been something like "Hire the handicapped." But by this time, I had sworn off online dating. Then it occurred to me one day: Looking at the Craigslist personals wasn't exactly online dating, was it? How could it be, when the headlines included things like DO YOU HAVE A LARGE CLITORIS?

I had only been on Craigslist one other time, and that was right before I'd moved out of my Georgian airplane hangar. I had to do something with the abandoned paraphernalia of five children, a husband, and various forgetful houseguests, but Jane and I couldn't even drag it out of the house.

Someone suggested I try the giveaway section of Craigslist, which turned out to be a good idea. So happy were the people who came to take my stuff; so happy was I to give it to them! Like the man who picked up a couple of dressers. He and his family had moved to Ohio to care for his dying mother-in-law, with whom the wife had never gotten along. But soon after they got there, the old woman had had a miracle recovery.

"She snapped right back, mean as ever," he said, shaking his head. "So I get up one morning and find the wife loading the kids into the van in their pj's. 'Get in,' she says. 'We're going home.' 'What about our stuff?' I say. 'We're leavin' it,' she says. 'Our furniture?' I say. 'Our clothes?'

" 'Don't worry,' she tells me, 'we'll find new things. Somehow we'll be provided for.' " He gave me a grateful look. "See? Sure enough, we are."

After this experience, Craigslist held a certain magic for me. If it could find those people free bedroom furniture, who knew what else it could do?

In the personals section I searched for the keyword *writer*—if Michael Chabon had decided to leave Ayelet Waldman, wouldn't this be the way to find him?—and there was just one hit, a forty-eight-year-old in Annapolis. The headline read THE PERFECT GUY? OR ANOTHER WACKY CL POSTER? YOU DECIDE. The post was a long, silly, but somewhat funny multiple-choice test by a guy who seemed a little arrogant about his assets and his requirements. There was a picture on the bottom of a man running on the beach. If this was him, arrogance might be overlooked.

You decide.

One hot, high-school-like week of e-mails later, I drove down to meet "Brett" (the name he gave me never seemed to me to be his real name) at a harbor-front tavern in Annapolis. Even before I hit the football traffic for the US Naval Academy, I was a nervous wreck. At five minutes before two, I called the number I had for him and said I was going to be late.

"No problem," he said. "There's no other way to get into town, so just relax." I had heard his voice once before, during our pre-date phone call. It was pleasant and deep, with a level-headed Midwestern tone.

About a half-hour of high blood pressure later, I pulled into a postcard-perfect enclave of shops and restaurants. Beneath a clear blue sky sailboats floated on the bay, and, despite the crowds of tourists, I found a parking spot near the appointed spot. I was scanning the sidewalk when I heard a voice from behind. "Marion?"

He, too, was ridiculously picturesque, in the manner of Joe Fiennes in *Shakespeare in Love*, a movie that had been getting me in trouble since the day it came out. Intense eyes, tanned skin, high cheekbones, white teeth, and full lips. Dark hair with a few strands of gray. Black jeans, motorcycle jacket.

He was smiling at me. "Do you want to sit inside or out? What do you want to drink?" Since I couldn't seem to think of an answer (I was so stunned by his beauty I had lost the power of speech), he ordered a couple of Dark and Stormies. I don't blame the rum for what happened next; hormones were working in my brain like Tide in a washer, rinsing my skull clean of all rational abilities as my body entered the acute phase of the agitation cycle.

I already knew a lot about Brett from the e-mails that had preceded our meeting. He lived alone on a sailboat and had driven race cars professionally for years. He was from Texas and was a Dallas Cowboys fan, as I and my sons had become during our Austin years. His high school graduation had been held in Cowboys Stadium, a detail whose power over me I cannot fully explain.

He was recently divorced after thirty years of marriage to the woman who had been his college girlfriend. After he quit racing and they'd sent the kids to college and moved to Baltimore, an aggravated case of empty nest took them down. By aggravated, I mean that his wife had gone back to graduate school, gained a lot of weight, and stopped paying attention to him while he had an affair with her best friend. She got the house, he got the sailboat.

In any case, Brett certainly wasn't hiding any of the awkward details of his situation. His Craigslist ad had announced that he'd only ever been with two women: his wife and her best friend. I'd thought it was a joke. It also said he didn't want to date anyone who weighed more than 130 pounds, and that he would prefer to see a married woman. Why a married woman, I asked him at some point, and he clarified for me that it meant he didn't want love, romance, or even a real relationship . . . just a low-overhead, no-strings-attached roll in the hay.

It's a little unbelievable that I even wanted to meet the guy given all these red flags. But now that I had, red flags meant nothing to me.

When I did try to keep up my end of the conversation, I only talked about things so stupid that I was forced to trail off two sentences into the thought. Later I saw all my abortive conversation topics listed on a dating site titled "Things Men Hate to Talk About."

1. Past relationships
2. Other dates
3. Celebrities
4. Religion
5. Politics
6. Antiques
7. Money
8. Fashion
9. Gardening
10. Marriage

I believe I avoided Gardening and Antiques, but added a few personal selections, such as Possible Reasons Why You Won't Like Me, and Diseases I Do and Don't Have. Jesus God Almighty. Miraculously he did not get up and leave, or even appear to be put off. He suggested we get the check and go for a walk.

After several blocks of meandering, we sat down on a bench and he started telling me about the time his family dropped anchor in Guatemala and he was mistaken by the militia for a local and taken into custody. More engrossing than the story was the way we were staring into each other's eyes. His were sparkly and brown; mine, he was soon to tell me, were very blue.

"Would you mind if I kissed you?" he asked matter-of-factly.

"No," I said. "I wouldn't."

He took me in his arms and put his mouth on mine, and I guess he must be the devil because even right now, given everything that's happened since, I would start that kiss over again in a second. Electricity, chemistry, physics—all the forces of nature unleashed their fury at the intersection of our jaws. We weren't just kissing like teenagers; we were kissing like insane teenagers on Ecstasy. When it ended, maybe ten minutes later, I was basically lying across his lap, our arms and legs were tangled, and people passing across the street looked alternately horrified and amused.

At some point, we stood up and floated back toward the harbor. We walked with his arm around me, all of our limbs now moving in effortless rhythm. When we reached the water, he pointed to a boat that he said wouldn't make the turn it was trying to round; momentarily, the crew's difficulties proved he was right. He went on talking about sailboats, sailboat accidents, and sailboat insurance. I was spellbound.

We sat on another bench, this one overlooking the water, and he started to kiss me again. I took off my sunglasses and put them on the bench beside me. That was the last I would see of those sunglasses, and I didn't even care. I was glad to leave them there, a memorial to abandon.

He had told me earlier that he would have to leave at 5:00 p.m. to go to a friend's kid's football game back down in Northern Virginia. Now it was very close to 5:00, he apologetically pointed out. I couldn't imagine at that point that he would really go, or that he wouldn't take me with him. A high school football game? Don't they have motels in Annapolis? But he was looking at his watch and heading to the parking area. It seemed we were going with Plan A.

Two motorcycles were parked next to each other. He asked me to guess which one was his, the blue one or the red one. I said the blue, but it was the red. Perhaps this was my big mistake.

Or maybe he had somehow determined that I weighed 132.

On the ride home, I could have driven to Kankakee and not have known it. It was a damn miracle when I saw a sign that said I was coming into Baltimore. I had been on the phone to Sandye the whole time, raving about the kiss—how it was like heaven, like heroin, like a perfect poached egg on toast. Sandye seemed to enjoy my elation to some extent, but entered a plea for caution. "You know how you are," she said.

When I got home I had a drink and a cigarette and anything else I could find in the house to bring me back to earth. It didn't work. I had to call Ken right away, and a couple other friends, and then I went on and told the story to the next dozen people I encountered, even a few I was meeting for the first time. Some were endeared to me instantly; others have never spoken to me again. I also told the story to my creative writing students at school, which many of them mentioned as a positive in their post-semester course evaluations.

Some people I was scared to tell, such as my sister, who was well aware of my behavior when under the sway of mad lust. We had had a tug-of-war with a sleeping bag that nearly turned into a fistfight shortly after I met Tony in New Orleans; she could not believe I was throwing myself at a gay man with such utter and humiliating flagrancy.

Even though I was vindicated then, I held off burbling to her this time—at least, for a while. I also avoided telling Jane about Brett. Everything that had happened up to that point in my new dating career had been harmless and basically nonsexual: Uncle Norm, Arnie, even Humberto the Tortilla Man. But the thing with the race-car driver felt red-hot and dangerous—PG-13 on its way to X. It had quite a ways to go before it would be something in which one would involve one's fourth-grade child.

Meanwhile, Crispin had recently notified me that he and his girlfriend, an Italian-Catholic woman who was an aide in a school for autistic kids, were going to take Jane to the Philadelphia Zoo for the day. I was blind-sided by this development and handled it badly, freaking out at the infamous Hereford Exxon. Once her father and I were screaming at each other, Jane burst into tears. She could not bear even one more second of conflict between us.

Though I claimed it was because I had been peremp-torily notified at the last minute of the trip, which involved sleeping over at the girlfriend's house, it was obviously more than that. This would be Jane's first expe-rience of seeing one of her parents with a new romantic partner, the beginning of a new phase for our atomized family. This girlfriend had been in the picture for quite a while already, so the outing was not inappropriate. But it was enough new information for the moment. Brett would have to stay undercover.

No matter how crazy I was going in my head, my first e-mail to him was relatively restrained. "There was no traffic at all going home," I wrote. "Took forty min-utes—good thing, because my mind was hardly on the road. How was the game, and the rest of your night?"

"Broke down on the side of the road on the way back—just got in," he replied. "Thought about the kisses a lot."

Though his e-mails were less frequent than the first week—he said he was "having trouble getting to Gmail"—he was still flirting when he did. But then he wrote something troubling. "You have beautiful eyes, Marion. I have to say that the depth of them is a little frightening to me, coming from where I have been. It almost seems too easy to fall into them."

Uh-oh. It was starting already. I felt the floor beneath me begin to give. Soon I would fall through a trapdoor in my psyche to the place where crazy girls boil bunnies and make hang-up calls and stalk the Internet at 3:00 a.m.

Despite every single person I knew warning me not to, I wrote and asked when I would see him again. Then Wednesday morning I went to the mall before my yoga class. At the Clinique counter, I spent $108 dollars on antiaging cream. Just as I was stuffing my iPhone into my purse before entering the yoga studio, an e-mail arrived. It put a huge smile on my face.

I had recently forwarded Brett some of the funny messages I'd received from when I had a profile up on Match, the dramatic proposals of my ESL suitors. This inspired him to write one of his own:

marion,

your eye like beauty and mouth appreciates. Together we have fun much and play. For sure you and me absolutely lovers forever with great time and fun. All you must do is only tell me and I will be man for you. I make you happy and smiling all day long, marion. Please please let me meet out with you sometime soons! My mother want meet you too, she thinks you have smarts. How can't you see the niceness we can get? The big pennis in my pants want to make to love with you and you will always be liking it for always. I must have seen with you. please.
Bill

I was beside myself—not only because it was funny, but because I naively believed that he couldn't have written those things if he didn't feel some version of the sentiments described. But on the way out of yoga, going immediately for the phone, I found another e-mail.

This one said good-bye.

I am torn between wanting to see you again and wanting to stop before it is too late. My instinct says to stop and I have to follow it. If I don't now, I could end up stopping when it is much harder for us both, and we would both likely be hurt.

I was so wide open emotionally and physically after all that had happened, not to mention an hour and a half of hot yoga practice, this message hit me like a wrecking ball in the chest. I could barely get to my car. Through my tears I typed back on my phone: "Is this because I brought up the second date?"

Good thing I hadn't told my sister.

My friend Nancy Raynovich and her daughter Tess came into town for the weekend; I was unable to talk or think about anything but Brett. That kiss really was worse than heroin, and rejection was the cocaine that made the speedball. No matter how normal I might look on the outside, the truth is I was a sick, sick woman, and this guy was playing my mazurka.

I took my houseguests shopping in Hampden, a quintessentially quirky Baltimore area. Tess got a vintage gold gown to wear to her high school homecoming dance, and I bought two things for Brett, things that jumped off counters into my hands even though I had never conceived such items existed. One was a package of gum. On the back of the silver box a disclaimer read, "By accepting WANNA-HOOK-UP GUM, receiver agrees to enter into sexual relations (i.e., to "hook up") with giver. It is mutually agreed that relations are limited to acts of sex and do not include exchange of phone numbers, first or last name(s), or inner feelings about anything deep and meaningful. Void in France."

In a shop down the block, I found a card with a deep scarlet envelope. On thick, creamy stock it said DON'T BE A, beneath which was a line drawing of a chicken. The inside was blank. I paid for the card and right there at the counter wrote in careful cursive, *I will keep my eyes closed so you won't fall into them.* Then I put the gum in the envelope and went to the post office, before I myself chickened out.

Seventeen-year-old Tess was getting a very unusual impression of the romantic practices of older women, but she seemed to be enjoying it. I certainly was. It's a high point of bipolarity when you can take people on your manic ride with you.

The next weekend, now two weeks from our meeting in Annapolis, I was down in D.C. and I e-mailed Brett to suggest we meet for coffee on my drive home to talk things over. He was dubious, saying it was forty-five minutes out of my way. Finally we agreed to meet at a Starbucks he found on MapQuest that would be sort of in the middle.

Sometimes the Internet just doesn't know what it's talking about. There was no Starbucks in this devastated former mall; there were no retail outlets of any kind. Instead there were drug dealers, drug buyers, gang members, and immense black SUVs idling in odd places around the parking lot. I waited in my car.

Finally Brett showed up on his motorcycle, handsome and smiling as ever. He was perfectly friendly and normal in his greeting, much as he had been in Annapolis. He regretted leading me to this unwelcoming spot and suggested I follow him up the road until we found something suitable.

He got back on the bike and I got in my Yaris and we headed out. One of the first things we went by was a roadside motel, but he passed it up and pulled into a T.G.I. Friday's. It was only about 3:30 or so, but we didn't order coffee. He had a beer; I had a glass of wine. I tried to make a case. He was scared mainly because he was inexperienced, I said; he had no idea of the wide variety of arrangements people could have between marriage and a one-night stand. There was really nothing to worry about.

He was pleasant but stood his ground, and I began to feel sort of tenuous, overheated, and overexposed. "Maybe we should leave," I said.

"Yes," he said.

I had one more question. "Will we kiss in the parking lot?" I asked.

He laughed. "Let's go see."

The kissing started where the kissing in Annapolis left off and went about as far as you can go in the parking lot of a T.G.I. Friday's: a very, very frustrating place. I remember standing on his feet to even out our heights, every inch of our bodies touching through clothes and jackets. I lost all self-consciousness, all inhibition, all sense of my age and geographic location. I did not understand why we hadn't gone to that motel. He said he'd seen it, too, with a wistfulness that made no sense.

This kissing had to stop before we got arrested; anyway, I still had to drive back to Pennsylvania to get Jane. I said into his neck, "Are you going to tell me tomorrow that you can never see me again?"

"You never know with me," he said.

But actually you do.

Instead of just throwing him back into the big ocean he'd come from, I suggested we become friends. (Yay! More friends!) I read some of his creative writing and I sent him more books to read. We exchanged long e-mails every day; I usually wrote back to his instantly and then spent the next twelve hours awaiting his reply. I saved all

84

the e-mails in a folder—there were dozens, then hundreds—and reread the old ones while waiting for the new ones. Oh, I was hooked all right. By Halloween, I was back to wondering if we would see each other again.

Then suddenly he sent a flirtier e-mail, including some romantic song lyrics and mentioning kissing. When I hopped on that idea, he immediately backed off. Then, a little over a month after our first meeting, he announced that he was going into therapy and cutting off communications with me.

I decided to go into therapy, too. God knows I needed it.

"He'll be back," predicted Ken gloomily, and my son Hayes also weighed in on the matter. Though Hayes doesn't like to hear about my romantic exploits, I did find myself telling him a bit about Brett at some point.

"Oh my God, this guy is a total doucher," he said. "Forget about him, Mom."

Dreamboat or doucher? Or just another wacky CL poster?

You decide.

my life in therapy

While I was looking for a therapist, Ken had some news about Jack, the old friend he'd thought of fixing me up with back in February. Somehow in all these months I'd never completely given up on Jack, and asked Ken about him regularly between dating disasters. He had been off the market, having moved in with the woman he started dating back in March. Now that had ended, but unfortunately it was because he had recently gotten not one but two DWIs, leading to his losing his job. That did sound disturbing, but perhaps I would meet him anyway. So what if he had a breathalyzer on his car ignition? That could be a good thing, really. And someone being out of work had never stopped me before.

Ken said he'd give him a call, but the next evening came over looking pale beneath his perennial five o'clock shadow. He went straight to the kitchen and made himself a large rum and Coke. "I have bad news," he said.

"What? Jack already has another girlfriend?"

"No," said Ken. "He committed suicide."

I almost felt like I should go to the funeral. It would be our first date.

I have been in therapy on and off since seventh grade. But finding a therapist is not that much easier than finding a boyfriend, it turns out, and often "help" is not what you get.

The first psychiatrist that I ever saw was a Chinese-American woman with a son in my middle-school honors science class. I was sent to her after I wrote a long, spooky, cry-for-help type poem and swallowed a bottle of Excedrin. Getting a C in seventh-grade English (I think we would now call this a Jewish F) and a broken heart were the nominal causes of my nervous collapse, but I was also fascinated by mental illness as portrayed in books like *I Never Promised You a Rose Garden* and *The Bell Jar*. Ah, that Sylvia Plath. An ongoing danger to America's young romantics.

I would later realize that by limiting her responses to *Mmm-hmm* and tossing any question I asked back to me, my inscrutable therapist was following classic psychoanalytic procedures. At the time I thought she was one of the most annoying people I'd ever met. To her credit, she did manage to explain some of my self-esteem issues to my bewildered parents, who were as always just trying to help me. But the approximately fourteen doctors I was seeing at the time, including a speech therapist, were making me feel like the Elephant Man instead of just a somewhat chubby, slightly pigeon-toed, crooked-toothed, lazy-eyed preteen. The physical issues were all eventually fixed or went away on their own; my sad little soul would prove more intractable.

My teen years featured an old hippie psychologist my sister Nancy and I both saw, sometimes together. He said we could bring as many friends as we liked. He smoked bidis with us—Indian clove cigarettes rolled in leaves, very popular in the '70s—and hypnotized me to help me lose weight. One session involved me descending into an imaginary theater and visualizing my favorite food making an entrance on the spotlit stage. My favorite food was Dannon vanilla yogurt.

This, he explained, symbolized the male orgasm.

Also around this time I participated in a therapy group run by the mother of one of my high school friends in her basement. Grassroots-style group therapy was quite a craze back then, as were beanbag chairs, blond-veneer paneling, and shag carpeting, and everyone in our drama-club clique crowded down the stairs to the biweekly meetings, not wanting to miss a moment of the action. "Group," as it was known, was less like therapy than like an MTV reality show thirty years before its time, with all the parties to every slight and betrayal on hand for its confession, a domino-effect freak-out waiting to happen.

For example, when I stupidly messed around one night in a red Chevy Nova with Billy Donnelley (who was not my boyfriend, but who reportedly had porn-star-type anatomical equipment so often discussed by the boys in our crowd that it was difficult not to be curious about it), the big showdown occurred in a room that contained Billy, my boyfriend, me, all of our various siblings, other girls who had had indiscretions with Billy Donnelley, their menfolk, and our well-meaning, middle-aged group leader. Though Billy and I had not gone all the way, things were never the same again for me and my sweet, young boyfriend. Ah, those stupid '70s. Like Sylvia Plath, another wellspring of dubious inspiration and poor moral guidance.

In college, where I had developed a pioneering case of bulimia, I saw a Student Health psychiatrist who made me so mad with his insistence that my eating problem was really a sexuality problem that I threw my purse at him in our second session. (I think I was still a little edgy after the vanilla yogurt thing.)

Still, I wasn't completely discouraged, even though I continued to have only meager success on the therapy front. More obsessive love, more body-image issues, now throw in substance abuse . . . In my twenties, I practically drove a young Jungian therapist into another line of work. I was losing patience, too. At one point, I actually threatened to sue a guy who listened to me for a couple hours, diagnosed me with ADD, wrote me three prescriptions, and sent me a bill for $1,369. Multiple couples counselors threw up their hands at both my first and second marriages. When I started to believe one of my kids was a dangerously manipulative charmer who had everyone around him bewitched with his lies, I of course sent him to see a therapist as well. She called me after a few visits to tell me that I shouldn't worry about my son. Everybody lies a little! And he was so charming.

Unbelievably, none of these experiences had destroyed my faith in therapy, and so I set out once again to be healed, this time in the living room of an elderly, cadaverous, former Episcopal priest whose main advantage was that he was right in my neighborhood. On our first visit, he said he wasn't sure he could help me with my problems, since they were so severe. On our second visit, he decided he'd rather not hear the pages and pages of dreams I had written down at his suggestion (though they seemed at the very least to be full of lottery number picks). On our third visit, he pulled out his Bible and started reading aloud. When I called him the following week to cancel our next appointment, I got the impression I had barely beaten him to it.

When I re-injured a sprained ankle later that fall (I wish I could say it was sports related but in fact I am just tragically uncoordinated), Ken insisted I go to the emergency room. Against my better judgment—knowing from experience that there is nothing you can do for a sprain except rest, ice, compress, and elevate—I let Ken drag me to a Patient First urgent care center. While we were waiting I noticed a paperback copy of the book *Desire,* a memoir of sex addiction by Susan Cheever, on the chair beside me, atop a crocheted blue shawl. I picked it up to see if they had used a quote from the review I'd written of the book. They hadn't, and I put the book back. Who was the person who had left it there, I wondered. When a friendly-looking, blonde, blue-eyed woman gingerly carrying her hurt left arm in her right returned to claim her things, I told her I had looked at her book.

"Oh," she said. "I'm a therapist!" She obviously wanted to dispel the impression that she was reading it because she was a sex addict.

"And I," I quickly replied, "am a book reviewer."

She was taken away to have something more done to her arm. As I sat there, I thought about the woman, feeling more and more drawn to her. This, I was sure, was my therapist. So I sneaked down the hall and peeked in the cracks between the curtains of the treatment rooms until I found her. She and her attending physician looked up, surprised, as I boldly swept in and asked, "Can I have your business card?"

I saw Tracy on Tuesdays, right after my hot yoga class. We talked about my ex-husband, of course, whose anger and blame were still very live issues for me, and about my recent bad experiences with the race-car driver in Annapolis. This seemed to exemplify another disastrous element of my character: the power of good looks and good kissing to blow my circuits. One does get to a point in life where it's sort of exhausting, filling in the same old backstory, and then even more discouraging to realize how similar the new stories are. But Tracy was a good listener, neither a pushover nor a super-confrontational critic, and I never had to throw my purse at her once.

God knows I have always been too restless and impulsive and impatient for my own good, sometimes drastically so, and I have long suffered with the burning desire to climb out of my head and go someplace else, often with some sort of chemical assistance. While motherhood has made me a much healthier person—as it couldn't Sylvia Plath—it hasn't fixed every glitch. Tracy wouldn't be able to, either, but she did help me out of the post-marital pain pit and onto more solid ground. I miss her, which is more than I can say for most of my old pay-pals.

Just like love, therapy is always worth another try.

little sweetheart
of the boston strangler

Like so many therapists before her, Tracy had to be made
aware of my disturbing romantic history. My taste in men
has always been unusual, going beyond the standard pre-
dilection for "bad boys" into uncharted territory.

For example, my earliest memory of romance is an
attempt to initiate a pen-pal correspondence with jailbird
Albert DeSalvo, the Boston Strangler himself. It was 1967,
I was nine years old, and I had just read Gerald Frank's
true-crime bestseller, *The Boston Strangler.* (This was typi-
cal of my reading material at the time, consisting mainly
of books my mother had requested from the library for
herself.) What you may not realize is that DeSalvo was
never even charged with the thirteen killings he is associ-
ated with; he was in the pen for something else. And if
you had read the interview in this book, and found out,
as I did, about his horrible, sad childhood and marriage,

you'd probably want to write him a letter, too. (Too late; he was murdered in jail in 1973.)

I graduated from DeSalvo to the boys of the board-walk in my hometown of Asbury Park, New Jersey. When we were fourteen, my neighbor Donna Benoit and I both fell in love with a doltish hoodlum named Dave Reis. I can't remember what was good about him except his shoulder-length blond hair, which was very straight and shiny and hung in his face. He may have had a missing tooth. We found him on a particular bench where you could always meet guitar-playing ne'er-do-wells, and guitar was our bond. Good thing, as he was not much of a conversationalist. From him, I learned the opening bars of "Stairway to Heaven." Soon after, he stole my guitar.

Dave Reis was followed by Buddy West, who came in a set with his brother Bobby. Bobby was strawberry blond and freckly, Buddy, rawboned and hazel-eyed. They had an apartment on the top floor of a rattrap building called the Santander. This was an early experience of bad sex on a bare, possibly insect-infested mattress. Also, they stole cash from my father's desk drawer and steaks from our freezer. My sister dated Bobby, but Buddy was all mine.

An even less memorable seaside rendezvous was with The Guy with the Convertible that I Bailed out of Jail. I recall nothing about him except that the bail was $150.

Why was I like this? Perhaps it was my parents' fault for bringing me up in comfort and ease, with my own shag-carpeted bedroom, ballet and piano lessons, new clothes each fall, and family trips to Disney World. What were they trying to do to me? To rebel against their kindness and generosity, I pretty much *had* to seek malevolence and dysfunction, or simply spiritual and material impoverishment.

As an undergraduate, I completely lost my heart to my six-foot-six, curly-haired housemate Mitch, who had a cocaine problem and had suffered a nervous breakdown, but was the focus of my hopes and dreams and terrible poetry for many years. Also at Brown I met Jan, my first long-term boyfriend. Just as I had had my enthusiasm for the Boston Strangler, Jan had a fixation on Squeaky Fromme, spokeswoman for the Manson Family and would-be assassin of President Gerald Ford, and had even thought of a plan for springing her from jail.

Jan was devoted to bringing down the capitalist state by making free long-distance phone calls and robbing banks, both according to schemes he'd found in *Steal This Book*. For the bank-robbing, you went through old obituaries in the library to find a baby who would have been about your age if it hadn't died. You got this dead baby a Social Security card and some other ID, then used that to buy traveler's checks. You reported the checks lost, got replacements, then quickly cashed both sets at different banks, wearing a disguise for the security cameras. The whole thing made me a nervous wreck, so I was relegated to driving the get-away car, a copper-colored 1972 Olds Cutlass given me by my uncle Philip, who I hope is not reading this.

Eventually our revolutionary ideals led us to East Germany, where we could live among like-minded brethren. After several months of unbelievably dull and oppressive socialist living, we went to West Berlin, where we hoped to go to film school for free. By this time, I was so home-sick I missed the tollbooths on the New Jersey Turnpike, and started making plans to get out of there. Thirty-five years later, Jan still lives in Berlin being super-cool and disaffected. He makes art movies and documentaries.

I returned home to a ménage-à-fifteen that Sandye and Nancy were running down in Austin. It was then that I met David Rodriguez, an authentic Mexican-American street person, at an art opening. My friends and I were at the event for the free food, and in the months to come he would teach us many more ways to get things for free. Hopelessly in love, I hitchhiked with him to Colorado to a creative writing conference. He went to an outdoor concert where he was arrested while trolling around the grounds for pills people had dropped. When the police searched him, they found someone else's ID in his pocket—someone who was wanted for grand larceny in the town of Junction, Colorado, hundreds of miles away. I hitchhiked out behind the police car to spring him. Ultimately, he stole our stereo.

Over the years, I took several trips abroad with Sandye. These provided many opportunities for unsuitable liaisons, as word of a female American tourist passing through town with her easy virtue and her MasterCard will bring out the flower of any country's freeloading sleazebags. In fact, they're not all sleazebags—some are quite nice—and for this reason it is possible to think of yourself as doing charitable work overseas rather than just being taken advantage of by the uncircumcised.

For example, Dave and his friends were a group of on-the-dole Liverpudlians we met in a bar. They gave us cigarettes and took us to what seemed to be their home, a tent in a field outside Cambridge. Dave was sallow, hollow-cheeked, and so thin I feared I might accidentally suffocate him. Though he and his friends stole our camera right after we took the group photos, when I got home there was a letter suggesting he come to the States and live with me. In a trailer, he said.

Perhaps the biggest mistake I ever made was when I went with my bluegrass-loving college friends to the Fiddlers' Convention in Union Grove, North Carolina, in 1977. I didn't like bluegrass as much as they did, and I soon found live banjo and fiddle combined with very strong LSD to be a form of psychological torture. Even today I cannot hear bluegrass without experiencing a nerve-jangling acid flashback. However, this unpleasantness was dwarfed by my decision to sleep with a guy named Tim. I remember little about him except his first name, and that he looked something like Gregg Allman. I met him that evening when he fell into our bonfire. The rest of our romance is a blank until the next morning, when he failed to stumble all the way outside the tent for a pee and apparently mistook my sleeping bag for a large tree root.

By the 1980s, things had gotten rather grim. Eddie Gonzalez was my sister Nancy's first husband's friend from high school, and I think he may have been the original link in the chain that got us all doing intravenous drugs. Since Eddie is now many years dead of AIDS, I don't want to go on too much about his terrible complexion, his tedious conversation, or his addiction—all of these I was only too eager to share at the time. Even he was horrified by the stupidity of my crush on him.

As should now be clear, the apparent bizarreness of my first marriage must be seen in context. If Tony was a penniless, gay bartender who had recently lost his job as an ice-skating coach due to his drug problem, he was still a significant upgrade from his predecessors. Aside from his other charms, he was madly in love with me, and innately nurturing and domestic.

After his death, I repelled the advances of a gorgeous, wealthy, physically fit, and socially conscious doctor— yes, a millionaire MD. He wanted to take me to Hawaii and entertain me at his marble-floored mansion. I gave him no encouragement, though during a particularly screwed-up period, after his crush had petered out, I tried unsuccessfully to get him to write me a Vicodin prescription. During the same period, I rejected the marriage proposal of a perfectly nice single dad I'd been hanging out with for a few years. I was waiting for the appearance of my second husband, I suppose, whose complex combination of alcoholism, anarchism, anger, OCD, distrust of women, brilliance, and talents in the bedroom made him the romantic disaster of all time. Even the fact that he loved bluegrass couldn't stop me.

Having heard this entire backstory, plus a few more-recent updates, Tracy had me write down what I was looking for in a man. I took my assignment seriously and handed in several paragraphs. Tracy came back the next week with her assessment.

"You want to date yourself," she told me.

It was true: I had the checkered past, the dubious emotional health, the bohemian habits that I was historically attracted to, and I certainly shared my interests. I often treated myself less than nicely, which would keep me interested, and while I might not be ideal on the erotic front, no one was more efficient.

Unfortunately, still clinging to my multi-decade obsession with lost causes, I was not available.

Was there no way to just stop all this and be happy with my dear, affectionate housemates, Jane and Beau; my new and old friends; yoga and chardonnay; occasional re-screenings of *Shakespeare in Love*?

Not yet, anyway.

the ambassadress
of the white race

Despite Tracy's ministrations, I was still reeling from the calamity of the Doucher when on the first Tuesday in November, my food-writer pal Martha and I made our monthly outing to the happy hour held by a city magazine we both wrote for. I brought Jane and Martha brought her daughter Mary, since having them play together saved us each the cost of a sitter. They ran off to a less-crowded corner of the place while we struggled to get near the bar. Fresh from months of hot yoga, I had exhumed my black miniskirt and heels from their mausoleum.

On the way, I attempted to wriggle past a tall African-American gentleman with short, graying hair and the build of a retired NFL tight end. "Can I help you, baby?" he asked with amusement. "Do you need a glass of wine?" He was dressed in an immaculate three-piece suit with a pocket square. As he sized me up, his lips curved in a deep U shape, like a ladle. "I think I need to get to know you better."

Not long after we'd introduced ourselves, shouting to be heard and still smushed together by the crowd, J. Joshua Johnson asked me out. "Would you like to spend some time with me?" he asked, smooth as Southern Comfort. "Can I take you to lunch?"

I studied him skeptically.

"It doesn't have to be lunch! I'll take you to dinner, I'll take you to breakfast—I'll take you anywhere you want to go," he said, his dimples deep, his teeth glinting.

At this point I caught sight of Jane and Mary threading their way toward us. Jane explained that they couldn't get near the hors d'oeuvres and were starving. "Could we go sit down and order?" asked Mary.

"Well, sure," I said magnanimously, then called after them, "Hey! Split something!"

By this time, Martha had materialized at my elbow. I introduced her to my new friend. "He wants to take me to lunch," I told her. The two of them began debating restaurant possibilities. Martha, a food writer, voted for a fancy place in the Inner Harbor.

J.J. smiled. "Is that okay with you, beautiful? How 'bout this Friday?"

Well, it sounded okay to me, but it was also happening a little fast. I suggested we get in touch to confirm.

After his departure, some nearby ladies offered testimonials. A friend of his who owned a deli, clearly a nice Jewish girl like myself, leaned over to comment. "That went well, didn't it, dolling?"

"He's quite a smoothie," I said.

"Oh, he's a very nice man. You should definitely let him take you to lunch," she said.

"Go to lunch, yes, you'll have a lovely time," another woman, bosomy and blonde, counseled. "But no matter what, do not sleep with him for at least three weeks."

"Three weeks?" I said dubiously. I hadn't had sex in over a year, and that one time had been the relapse situation with my ex. Really, I hadn't had sex in almost two years.

"Three weeks!" she repeated firmly. She launched into some of the standard arguments for restraint.

"Okay," I said, "you're right. Three weeks." She rolled her eyes, as did several others around us. Sure, they were thinking; this woman is a desperate ho.

When I went to find Jane and Mary, they were seated at a candlelit table surrounded by half-empty plates and glasses. They'd had lobster macaroni and cheese, Caesar salad, garlic bread, and a couple of Shirley Temples. Now the waitress was on her way with cheesecake and a sundae.

"Whoa," I said. "That's quite a spread, girls." I looked around for Martha as I reached in my bag for my wallet, hoping she would split the bill.

"You know your friend in the suit?" said Jane. "J.J.?"

"Yeah?"

"Well he came and got the check, told us to order dessert, and paid for the whole thing."

"He even tipped the waitress," Mary added.

My eyes widened and my head swiveled toward the doors through which he must have exited, as if I'd see a twinkling trail of stars hovering above the white marble floor.

❧ ❧

The intervening days were filled with the usual prepa-rations and hysteria about what to wear. I ended up in brown wool wide-leg pants, a somewhat suburban low-cut shirt with metallic peacock feather designs on it, and high heels I couldn't walk in. But there are no high heels I can walk in, so what can you do.

I waited until Friday morning to get a manicure so it wouldn't get wrecked before the lunch, then ruinously scraped it getting into the car. By this time I was so wound up, I practically had a stroke driving downtown in the pouring rain, and another when I saw the price of the parking lot in the Inner Harbor.

A set of revolving doors led me from the monsoon into the smiling welcome of hostesses and coat-takers. The restaurant was warm and dry, with golden sconces glowing against the polished paneling and thick carpets to buttress my tottering heels. J.J. was waiting for me, as impeccably turned out as ever.

"You look beautiful, darlin'," he said. "I'm so glad you came. Order anything you want. Anything."

As we ate and sipped at balloon goblets of wine, I asked about his childhood. It sounded rough. Between his mother and father, he told me, they'd had twenty-three children. But the ghetto days were clearly over now. He took calls from people in the mayor's office during lunch. He heard from his daughter Josie, whose car had been towed up at Penn. Throughout the conversation, he sprinkled mention of a lot of cool-sounding things he owned—boats, beach houses, and such.

And he asked about me. Oh, me. You know, I'm just your standard ex-junkie AIDS widow. It is really hard to condense the story of my life into polite conversation, but I tried. "I hope hanging around with me won't ruin your reputation," I concluded.

"Oh, well. I have some issues in my past, too," he said,

smiling. "I'll probably tell you when we get to know each other a little better."

As we lingered, he asked if I'd ever dated a black guy. I told him about Brent, a tall, beautiful boy from Southern California I knew in New York in the early '80s. I didn't ask him if he'd dated white women. That would have been silly.

We had a warm but not messy kiss in the lobby of the parking garage (which, by the way, cost thirteen bucks an hour). I was winging those bills out the window as fast as I could, eager to get home and start Googling.

It wasn't easy, but LexisNexis finally got me to an old article in the *Baltimore Sun*. J.J. had been the leader of one of two groups of investors competing to take over a hotel project for the city—until his opponents leaked to the press that he was a convicted felon who had done time for attempted murder.

Some might have seen this as a discouraging development. I, however, was fascinated. I had to at least get the whole story.

The following Monday, J.J. stopped by my house after work in his vintage red Corvette, electrifying my neighborhood. I was cooking dinner for Ken's elderly parents and felt awkward asking him to join us. They would have assumed he was a new boyfriend—I'd never even had them over before—but inwardly I wondered whether it was because he was black. Would I be inviting him to stay if he were white? Was he wondering this, too?

"Oh, honey, you don't have to invite me to dinner. I don't even eat dinner. I'll just sit at the counter, and watch you cook for a while," he reassured me.

He certainly watched me. Watched every move. I felt like I was doing something much sexier than cleaning shrimp, as if my curves were highlighted like key passages in a text.

"You look like you know what you're doing in the kitchen," he commented.

"Oh, I'm sorry," I said again awkwardly. "This is so rude."

"Honey, I keep trying to tell you—I'm perfectly happy. Stop being so nervous. I adore you. Don't you adore me?" he asked.

I couldn't help laughing. "J.J., white people don't say 'I adore you' in situations like this. But theoretically, I adore you, too."

"Okay, then what are you doing Friday night?" he asked. "I think I have some free time then."

By now I'd waited long enough to get to the subject that was really on my mind. I confessed my to Internet snooping, and he sighed, then told me this story.

Back in his twenties, J.J. had owned a nightclub in D.C. with a partner. The partner had a girlfriend who was married to an abusive asshole, and they'd asked J.J. to do something about this dude for them. J.J. said Hell, no. They offered money. He told them it was a bad idea.

Not long after that, the partner called and asked J.J. to meet him at the mall. When J.J. had pulled into the parking lot, it was full of police cars. As they cuffed him, he learned there had been an unsuccessful attempt on the life of the man he'd been asked to kill. The wife was the initial suspect, but now he was under suspicion as well.

At the time of this unpleasant trip to the mall, J.J. was packing heat—necessary, he explained, because he was constantly carrying cash from the club. That didn't help his case. Nor did a phone call the wife had recorded in which they had discussed the idea. Long story short, he was convicted on circumstantial evidence, and both of them did time. "All-white jury in D.C.," he said. "What do you expect?"

Fortunately, he served five years of a thirty-five-year sentence and was paroled at age thirty. Having made the most of his time behind bars, he left the pen with a degree in business administration and a second wife (his first flew the coop after he got locked up, so he married the woman who taught college classes in the jail).

I was filled with outrage and sympathy and disbelief, but not the kind of disbelief where you actually don't believe. I did believe.

Friday night came. But before that, just a half-day before that, came my period. Tsunami style. I was in despair. How was I going to have sex for the first time in so long while I was hemorrhaging? Plus, considering I had already told him I have hepatitis C (part of the I-didn't-get-AIDS speech), there were not just aesthetic but health issues. Oh, Jesus Christ. Maybe I should just cancel the whole date.

But I'd already taken Jane up to her dad's in Pennsylvania. I'd put on my black pants and dark blue satin top with sparkly buttons. I'd lined my eyes and glossed my lips, and then I'd taken a little detour. I was standing in front of the refrigerator eating leftover collard greens with my fingers. I make great collards. I wondered dreamily whether I should bring him a sample. Oh right, a Tupperware bowl of collard greens and maybe some Jheri-curl cream, too.

J.J. lived in a part of town I had not visited before. Once an elite neighborhood, it had then descended most of the way into hood-dom. Now it was on its way back up again. J.J.'s place was as close to a mansion as a row house could be, with arched windows and pillars and curved balconies. It was surrounded by a wrought-iron fence draped in chains and titanium locks. Letting me in was a complex procedure.

Inside was a world of wonders.

There was room after room with walls painted in dark jewel tones and windows cloaked in thick velvet curtains. Each room contained a certain type of item, displayed on shelves and pedestals and in backlit glass cases. The first was Buddhas: golden, wooden, jade, stone, each with its hands in the classic mudra, its face wearing a meditative smile. Next was hourglasses. Some were tiny. Some were waist-high. Some were Victorian, others seemingly Egyptian.

After that, we came into a sort of living room, or at least the first room with couches and chairs. It featured models of clipper ships and framed oil paintings hung almost edge to edge.

Could a straight man really live here? A straight, single, black ex-con? It seemed more like some obscure museum in an outlying arrondissement of Paris than a home. But wait, there was more: Out back, in addition to the Vette I'd already seen, there was a vintage Bentley, a huge, brand-new SUV, and a gleaming Harley-Davidson the size of a twin bed in its own heavily secured trailer. Finally we went through an enormous basement filled with pallets of rugs, furniture, paintings, and God knows what else.

J.J. explained that after he'd gotten out of jail, he had a little trouble landing a job, so he'd entered various fields of self-employment, antiques dealer and real estate agent among them.

Perhaps there had been others.

After a series of winding staircases through media rooms and guest quarters, we arrived at the level of the royal boudoir. The bed was covered in lustrous brocade and meticulously arranged satin throw pillows. One wall of the room was made entirely of stained-glass windows. Another was a plasma television. And from the midnight-blue ceiling were suspended a half-dozen life-size golden mermaid statues.

I had to tell him I had my period. I really did. But first, maybe I should have a drink. He made me a pink concoction in a black martini glass in his marble kitchenette while I sat at his computer, trying to get us a dinner reservation and staring down my own cleavage, which waited patiently between dark blue satin lapels. I launched into a short, nervous speech about my period and how I'd almost canceled our date. He told me not to worry about it. "Let's just go to dinner, darlin'," he said.

Out in the vehicle storage yard, I went to climb into the SUV. Here we ran into a little problem. There was one thing J.J. insisted on, he said. I was absolutely forbidden to open my own car door. Every single time I got into or—much more annoying—out of a car with him, I had to wait until he came and opened the door for me. "What if," he said, "you go hopping out of the car onto the sidewalk and somebody snatches you up before I even get there?"

"What the hell are you talking about?" I said. We had definitely grown up in different neighborhoods. But I had to let it go or we were never going to get to dinner. So I did. For the moment.

At dinner, I realized that I was noticing the race of each of the people that served us—most of them were black men—and wondering what each made of us as a couple. Did they think J.J. was cool for being with me? Did they think I was cool for being with him? Could I have been having any less cool thoughts than this? At some point J.J. told me that the people he worked with were cheap Jews, and in my uncoolness this actually made me feel better.

By the time we returned to his house I was drunk, which made me more relaxed about the whole megillah with getting in and out of the car, and before I knew it I was up there with the flying mermaids. It was my first time in so long, and I wanted it to be special and perfect. I wanted it to erase my ex-husband and the Doucher and all my self-doubt, but more likely it was just going to be an unsexy mess.

My date, bless his heart, seemed to feel that with enough bath towels and condoms we could negotiate the sidewalk sale on body fluids.

His handling of the situation was nothing if not gallant. He murmured compliments about my soft skin and my nice stomach; he didn't even mention the damn tattoo of my husband's initials, and though this was probably an abbreviated version of his usual lady-pleasing routine, it was still nice. It did feel strange to be with someone other than my husband, but I tried not to dwell on it.

However, as the action continued, I was having a tough time interpreting exactly what phase of arousal he was in. He kept his eyes closed mostly, and when it was over, I was unsure whether he'd had an orgasm. Was I just out of practice? Should I do something about this? Apparently not, since he was already cleaning up the towels.

Later, lying sleepless and distraught beneath the flying mermaids, I wondered if perhaps he took Viagra, and that's what made it seem sort of odd. At fifty-five, J.J. was the oldest guy I'd ever slept with; maybe it was different with this age group. I'd have to ask Ken, I decided.

I looked over at him, now seemingly fast asleep, and started worrying about my usual bed partner, my beloved miniature dachshund. What could he possibly be thinking, now that it was three-thirty in the morning and I hadn't come home? I pictured him staring at the front door, his head tilted to the side. I would have left but I knew I couldn't get through the security system on my own.

At 5:00 a.m., I ventured a delicate toss-and-turn maneuver. "You all right, baby?" he asked. When I explained that I had to go home to my dog, he put on a pair of pajama pants and padded downstairs to undo all the bolts and padlocks and let me out. We had a muted, predawn farewell. He did not insist on following me to the car to open the door.

Both of the next two weekends he told me he might be able to see me. Both times, I assumed this meant he would see me. But never did he take my calls or answer my texts on a weekend night. I expressed my irritation about this in carefully worded e-mails and phone calls. He said he would try to do better.

I said something about what I expect from a boyfriend.

"Am I going to be your boyfriend?" he wondered, genuinely surprised.

"Well, I don't know," I said. "I kind of thought so, I guess."

The second Saturday night I sat with a girlfriend at a bar not far from his house, at first expecting he'd be joining us any minute; later, sending plaintive, drunken text messages. I was beginning to grasp, though he never explicitly said this, that I might not be his only girl. I might, for example, be a replacement trying out for the recently vacated number-seven spot.

We had sex one other time, sort of like makeup sex, though we hadn't exactly had a fight, at my house at lunchtime on a weekday. As we headed upstairs, I realized this would be the first time I'd been with a man in my postmarital bedroom, the incident with Humberto notwithstanding. J.J. admired the clerestory windows, the framed photographs, my mother's collection of Herend china animals arranged on the dresser. I flipped the little blue dog to show him its clever gold penis. Then he asked me for some hangers, and spent about five minutes removing the many layers and accessories involved in his fancy work costume, carefully hanging each of them in the closet.

Having thrown my jeans and T-shirt on the floor in a matter of seconds, I lay on the bed in my black underwear, watching.

The sex situation was as mystifying as the first time. There seemed to be no dramatic arc of any sort—no rising action, no suspense, no climax, no denouement. It seemed it could go on forever, really. This was not necessarily a good thing. And Ken said not to bring up Viagra.

The next weekend was Thanksgiving, my first big holiday in Baltimore. J.J. had plans that he never really clarified, but he called me on the holiday from a place where he was getting his car windshield fixed. I wondered if he'd been shot at. In between yelling instructions to the repair guy, he said he'd like to stop by before he left town.

"Well," I said, "my sons are home from college. Would you like to meet them?"

"Sure," he said, which I didn't expect. I hung up the phone and turned to my sons, side by side on the couch, watching the Dallas Cowboys game.

"Boys," I announced casually, "this guy I'm seeing is going to stop in before we go out to dinner."

"You're seeing someone?" asked Hayes.

"Yeah, dude, she's seeing some black guy; didn't she tell you?" his younger brother Vince replied.

"And he's coming over? Is it, like, serious?" Hayes asked.

"Oh, I don't think so, honey."

I was sitting at my desk in the front room when J.J. pulled up to the curb.

"Guys," I called. "My friend is here." One of the highlights of the whole relationship for me was the looks on my sons' faces when they saw J.J. get out of the Bentley. He was wearing a black leather Stetson hat, black tailored shirt and pants, softly gleaming black boots. He was blinged to the gills and really, the theme song from *Shaft* might as well have been playing in the background as he crossed the street.

"Holy shit, Mom," Hayes said.

A week or so later, I had planned a dinner date with J.J. and my D.C. friends, Jim and Jessica and Judy and Lou. I was feeling unsure about the plan, but not unsure enough to cancel. Perhaps the timing was off for the friend introductions. Then things got called off at the very last minute when Lou had emergency heart surgery.

When I called J.J. to bring him up to speed on these developments, he didn't seem to want to settle on an alternate plan. "You probably need to go down to D.C. and be with your friends," he said.

I hadn't even thought of that. "Not today, anyway."

"Well, maybe we can make this work some other time, then." As usual there was all kinds of noise in the background and it was hard to communicate. "I can't really talk right now," he said, "and you don't seem to be reading between the lines. I'll call you later."

"Okay," I said, hanging up slowly and staring at the words CALL ENDED on the screen. Read between *what* lines? Didn't we have a date? I didn't understand.

I decided to take his advice and drive to D.C., where I found my friends not only no longer in the hospital but heading to a French bistro for dinner so the heart-surgery patient could recount his story with the proper accompaniment of butter and alcohol. As I gazed out at the snowflakes drifting slowly down onto the sidewalks of our nation's capital, basking in the glow of good wine and old friends, a text from J.J. popped up on my phone. *I will call to reschedule.*

But that was the last I heard of J. Joshua Johnson, my knight in shining bling, or he of me. One way or another, our three weeks were up.

dear answer lady

1. freaking thanksgiving

One of my day jobs during this happy-go-lucky dating period was writing a monthly advice column for a national women's magazine. Obviously, I had a voluminous store of past mistakes I could draw on for instructional purposes. Furthermore, my position as a national moral resource was helping to bolster my growing determination not to run around town acting like an alcoholic, manic-depressive slut. An advice columnist needs to keep up appearances. Particularly, say, during the holidays, though I was well aware that they are the hardest time of year to pretend one is coping at all.

Let's take another look at that first Baltimore Thanksgiving of mine. Unsurprisingly, I had felt a little puny about it: I was an orphan, I was single, my thing with J.J. was pretty dubious, and I'd agreed to let Crispin take Jane to his mother's for Thanksgiving dinner. Hayes and Vince would be home, but given their terrifying and indiscriminate hunger, their passion for Chick-fil-A, Chipotle, and cheese steaks, my usual frenzy of gourmet preparations looked like a bad bet. How would I prove that I was a good mother and a decent human being?

Once, I had firmly believed these things were measured in ergs. The amount you loved your family could be rated week by week, or day by day, a kind of Standard & Poor's index of parenting value.

$$\frac{\text{Number of family members (miles driven + missing items located)}^2}{\text{Total hours spent in kitchen and laundry room}}$$

By the time poor Jane was born, I had let things slip a bit. I was less inclined to volunteer as a chaperone for school field trips, to enforce household rules that entailed climbing a flight of stairs, or God forbid, to throw a Frisbee.

And now, freaking Thanksgiving. Was there some way out of cooking for three days and cleaning up for another two, with a twenty-minute break between for the ravening stampede? Or should I hide my tears in my dead mother's favorite creamed pearl onions and carry on bravely? Tell me, Answer Lady, what to do.

Signed, Burnt Out in Baltimore.

Dear Burnt,

While there is an argument for the comfort of ritual in the face of chaos and crisis, this argument is usually made by those not responsible for producing these rituals. Often, the bereaved, the abandoned, the ill, and the otherwise beleaguered are tired. Very tired. Too tired to spell the word ritual, much less enact one. Also, you'd be amazed at how strongly you feel people's absence when their actual chairs are empty. But there is good news. They serve Thanksgiving dinner in restaurants. Get on the Internet and make a reservation, for God's sake.

2. chicken soup for dina lohan

Until you end up with a helpless infant on your hands, the seriousness of first-time parents looks ridiculous. Once there, you instantly grasp the problem: Your child could be hurt in any one of 2.3 million ways, 1.9 million of which would be your fault. It could even die—an unlikely prospect that will occur to you more than once a day. On the other hand, you could die and it could live. If you think you have little control now, wait 'til you're dead.

Should both of you survive, the seeds you plant with your early parenting will shape its entire future psyche, so if it turns out to be a criminal, a tyrant, a public disgrace, or just a miserable person, you will be Dina Lohan, a woman widely believed not only to have caused her daughter Lindsay's problems with drugs, alcohol, and the law, but to have capitalized on them.

Indeed, there are grounds for concern. The question is how to translate that anxiety into action.

I became a mother in my late twenties, which was in the late '80s. I lived in Austin, Texas, where I had fallen in with an enclave of New Age earth-mother vigilantes. We labored without drugs, breastfed for eighteen months minimum, used only cotton diapers, and made baby food from scratch. My older son Hayes had no sugar until after his first birthday, and was never left with a babysitter until then. If babies were not allowed at an event, I didn't go either. Sorry, baby-haters. Your loss.

Hayes's room, his toys, his stroller, his car seat—everything was chosen with consideration. Every decision, from immunizations to nap schedule to toddler disciplinary style, was the result of research and discussion. Television—NO! Black-and-white geometric mobiles—YES! Weaning and toilet training were studied like epistemology and calculus. And take it from me, you'll never run out of conversation with friends and strangers alike if your child uses a pacifier, as Hayes did. This is something people really, really want to put in their two cents on, whether they see it as a moral failing, a developmental problem, or a gateway addiction. As a writer, I had a whole cottage industry going with pacifier-related articles and radio broadcasts.

When Vince was born two years after his brother—at home on tie-dyed sheets, with a midwife who took the placenta away in a yogurt container—I raised him approximately the same way. By this time, however, I had furtively acknowledged the usefulness of Pampers, TV, and even baby formula in certain situations. As time went on, privileges long awaited by his older brother came early to Vince, starting with late bedtimes and PG-13 movies (PG-9, it turns out), and continuing through cell phones and unsupervised girlfriend visits. (Put a box of condoms in the bathroom and get an unlimited text-messaging plan.)

At the advanced age of forty-two, I ended up back in the ugly white bra with Velcro-closing cups, thanks to that baby-freak Crispin, who didn't think his two and my two were enough.

Nursing was about the only way Jane's babyhood resembled that of her older brothers. Breast pump; no way. Cloth diapers; ha. I'm not exactly certain when she started solid food, as her siblings were giving her french fries even as they taught her to play Grand Theft Auto on the PlayStation. She designed her own nap schedule; I left weaning and toilet training to her as well.

Then what happened? Oh, you know—the usual idyllic childhood, including substance abuse, delinquency, and felony charges among the family members (cemetery desecration, car chases, ski trips gone bad), followed by marital war and divorce. Not quite as cataclysmic as her brothers' dead-father script, but not what you wish on your five-year-old.

Without a doubt Jane has a Leftover Mom—lazy, lax, full of excuses, and in her mid-fifties, for God's sake. But with exhaustion has come a certain wisdom. I have observed children born of super-strict parents, helicopter parents, soccer moms, potheads, churchgoers, and people who have staff members perform 75 percent of their parental duties. I have seen enough mental effort to solve the serious troubles of the human race poured into minor child-rearing decisions. And for those who decide differently: jihad!

I do not deny that there are certain minimum requirements for safety, nutrition, and hygiene. But very few styles of parenting actually blow it in this respect. The bigger problem is that there are too many unhappy, stressed-out, exhausted parents who get little pleasure from parenting and are, in fact, about to snap. This snapping can go in many different directions, and none of them is good.

The thing that gets undervalued in the quest to do everything right is the need to take off some of the pressure. No matter how hard you try, you're going to have bad days—you'll make mistakes—and the best thing you can do is forgive yourself and move on. The reason anyone gets through a day that starts with whining, back-talk, shouting, curses, something wrong with these eggs, go live with your father, worst mother in the world, don't touch me, don't talk to me, cracked juice glass, awful radio station, enslavement to utter bitch, slammed door, silence, and welcome to Tuesday! is because they let it go.

Jane and I usually rely on a simple hand on the knee to say it all.

Your inner peace and strength are your child's great-est resource. This is not bullshit. When you're okay, they're okay. All the parenting micromanagement in the world doesn't change the thing that has the biggest effect on your kids: who you really are, in your heart and soul. That is the sky. Everything else is just the weather, the passing clouds.

3. mr. turkey

My parents had a long history of dining out for Thanks-giving. My mother was a golfing, blackjack-playing, martini-drinking sort who had little to do with cooking, sewing, or other domestic arts. Throughout my childhood, we ate Thanksgiving dinner at the Hollywood Golf Club in Deal, New Jersey; this club was essentially my parents' place of worship. Both my sister and I were eventually married there, and we scattered my mother's ashes on the ninth hole. The best thing about Thanksgiving at the club—other than the fact that it saved my mother from having to contemplate the creaming of pearl onions (or even the defrosting of the Birds Eye version)—was the magnificent centerpieces they assembled: towering cornucopias of nuts, fruit, chocolates, and candles in the shape of Pilgrim children that made my sister and me twitch with acquisitive longing.

Once I left home, I did things rather differently. I cooked myself silly every Thanksgiving, even during my early vegetarian years, and on through the ages of brining and turducken and pumpkin pie made from actual shaved pumpkin, according to *Gourmet* magazine (a multiday disaster; Answer Lady says stick to the canned). This particular rebellion of mine was just fine with my mother. She would come clear across the country if necessary, always bringing her signature contribution: the centerpiece, a creation known as Mr. Turkey.

Mr. Turkey consisted of a simplistic red felt turkey head, a black bead eye on either side, that could be attached to the butt end of a pineapple with straight pins.

You laid the fruit on its side so the leaves took the place of tail feathers and . . . ta da!

Even though the S-shaped seams of the neck were glued together and it could have been a preschool art project, I am quite sure my mother did not make the turkey head herself. Perhaps it was a gift from one of the ladies at the bridge table. When the eye fell off, we drew one on with a Sharpie. It had a certain outsider-art-meets-Lillian-Vernon charm, and it was at the center of my table every year, always surrounded by a flock of hand-carved apple swans I learned how to make from a chef friend in my early twenties. But this year, acts of daughterly one-upmanship had no audience, and peeling turnips, mashing potatoes, and rubbing butter into cold, pimply bird skin held little appeal. I looked on the Internet and, by God, dozens of restaurants in Baltimore were vying to get my business. I was nervous when I called a hotel dining room near my house and may have given the poor reservation clerk a little more backstory than was required. "I didn't ask why, hon," she said finally. "Just what time."

We had found Mr. Turkey up in the closet next to the wrapping paper after my mother died, his edges rotting from years of seeping pineapple juice. Nonetheless, I took him to the restaurant with us and stuck him on the bottle of Nouveau Beaujolais that was sitting on our table when we arrived. From there, all I had to do was eat, drink, converse with my sons, and give my credit card to the waiter. There was a huge buffet of food, and the boys piled their plates with salmon and roast beef and ham, claiming they had never liked turkey. Really? Well, thank God I hadn't spent half a day cooking the damn thing.

4. trivial pursuits

What with my weird, low-energy Thanksgiving Day having been such a success, I was developing a new appreciation for the wisdom of my own parents' credit-card-based approach to child rearing. Christmas was on the way, and suddenly I saw a detour around the shopping, cooking, decorating, cleaning, and socializing that so filled me with dread. I got right back on that Internet and booked two nights in a double room in a hotel on the beach in Fort Lauderdale for Hayes, Vince, Jane, and me.

We got up Christmas morning, flew to Florida, spent three un-fun hours waiting in line to rent a car in the airport, then picked up our Christmas dinner from the only restaurant open at 9:00 p.m., a Subway we passed on the way to the hotel. But as soon as we were ensconced at the Beachcomber, we unwrapped our sandwiches, then opened our gift: Trivial Pursuit Family. We played it until the sun rose over the Atlantic, which we couldn't actually see from our discount room overlooking the parking lot, but no one seemed to mind.

New Year's Eve I went down to D.C. and saw those heart-surgery-having / gourmet-food-eating friends of mine, who assembled each year for an over-the-top feast: 7 hours, 14 courses, 200 plates, glasses, and utensils, 8,000 bottles of wine, and a truly infinite number of calories. I may never get over the drinkable part of the dessert course: a chocolate shot layered with lavender-infused milk.

And that isn't the only thing I could not get over, apparently. A couple of days after I got home, I received an e-mail from long-lost Brett, unheard from for several months, who wondered in a single sentence if I was going to watch the Ravens in the NFL play-offs. It took me a while to comprehend that he was asking if he could come to my house to watch the game.

My house? Are you kidding? Did I have the only TV in the state of Maryland? Why would he do this? I didn't know then, and I don't know now. All I could think of was this Hollywood joke I heard years ago. After a difficult day, a struggling actor returns to his neighborhood and is shocked to find a horde of police cars and fire trucks surrounding the smoldering remains of his house.

"This is a crime scene, sir; you're going to have to move on," one of the officers orders him.

"But I live here!"

"You mean this is your house?" the officer asks in a more sympathetic tone.

"Yes! What happened?"

"Well," the cop says, "it seems that your agent came by earlier today, and while he was here he attacked your wife, assaulted your children, beat your dog, and burned the place to the ground."

The actor's jaw drops in disbelief. "My *agent* came to my *house?*"

There is a chance to spare myself some humiliation here. I don't have to tell you that I made a Ravens-theme supper consisting of purple coleslaw (the team color) and crab cakes (Baltimore's favorite food) and lemon rice. I could omit the Dark and Stormies (of course he didn't remember this is what we drank on our first date), or the fact that I got my toenails painted purple as well. I could just answer the questions you are most interested in. Did we have sex? No. Did we get past first base? No, although at his boyish suggestion, we made out every time the

Ravens scored. There were three touchdowns and a field goal in the first quarter alone. At a certain point, the frustration began to outweigh the thrill.

> Him: Why do you put up with me? This can't be fun for you.
> Me: I just have an intuition about us, I guess.
> Him: Is your intuition ever wrong?

Just a couple e-mails were required to wrap up this phase—he said he just wasn't ready, and I said, you know, I'm starting to believe you. A month later, on Valentine's Day, my intuition told me to look on Craigslist. Yes, his original post was up again. "The perfect guy? Or another wacky CL poster. You decide." This caused another short round of e-mails. I never saw the ol' dreamboat again, but it was not until October that communication ended completely.

After months of silence, a final volley of messages resulted in a plan for a one-year-anniversary meeting on the famous bench in Annapolis. Several days before the rendezvous, his messages included mention of a bothersome sore throat. My intuition told me this sore throat would worsen, and the date would be canceled.

My intuition was getting better all the time.

the five guys
you meet in hell

1. the russian spy

In February it snowed about four feet, schools were closed for two weeks, and everyone in the city was stuck in the house. This was a great time for me. When I lived in Pennsylvania, a serious snowstorm meant days of isolation, until I could get someone to come plow our quarter-mile driveway. For entertainment, I had a house-ful of bored, hungry children and piles of soaking wet snow gear. Usually the satellite would go down too, so no television. Finally, after clearing the parking lots of the Wal-Mart, the Taco Bell, and the elementary school, the snowplow would come to my house. Hours after they had left with half my mortgage, the snow would blow right back into the path they had cleared. It had gotten to the point where I had a morbid fear and hatred of snow.

But now, in the joyous city of Baltimore, I had no driveway, my neighbor shoveled my sidewalk, and he and everybody else around here were giving potlucks and parties during this unscheduled two-week winter holiday. It was like World War II in France, when they figured they might as well just drink all the champagne in the cellar since God knew what would happen next.

Ken lost power at his house and had to come stay with us for a few days. I met Pam, a young artist/mom who lived across the back alley and plied her with gløg; she became my closest friend in the neighborhood. Then, just when we were about to run out of booze, some kids found the bottle of Sailor Jerry rum Ken had dropped when he fell into a snowdrift on his way to my house. And returned it!

The only negative about Snowpocalypse was that my being stuck in the house for so long caused a brief relapse into online dating. My old Greenfields pal Arnie had recommended a free site called OkCupid, and one snowy afternoon I sailed out there.

I was drawn to the photos and ironic comments of a guy named Mike. In our exchanges he turned out to be a funny fellow with a Russian accent who had emigrated to Baltimore as a thirteen-year-old. He was single with grown children—in fact, one of his kids was taking the New York bar exam. But wait. Mike was purportedly around forty. How could he have a twenty-five-year-old? As a young immigrant boy of fifteen, he told me, he had impregnated the secretary of his middle school and ultimately had two children with her. He lived with her for years but they had never married.

I thought this was quite a story, and I like a story. So I agreed to meet him for a bagel, though during our phone conversations I had become concerned about his compulsive ending of most sentences with an awkward, forced chuckle: "... heh heh heh. *Anyway* ..."

I sat at the table by the window at Greg's Bagels, watching as various elderly and infirm people who couldn't possibly be him entered. I thought the guy who rolled up in the wheelchair with his atrophied legs folded into a half-lotus was one of them until he greeted me.

"Marion! You're just like your picture!"

Because there was no possible correct expression of my own reaction, I said little as we proceeded to the counter to order our bagels. I was quite flustered by the whole procedure. Should I carry his coffee for him? Move the chair next to me out of the way? Should I let him pay for me? Well, no problem with that one, because they didn't take cards and he had no cash. He insisted we go to the ATM afterwards so he could pay me back.

"Oh, come on—five bucks, big deal," I said, wondering how exactly we would go to the ATM. Everything was awkward in my stunned, unprepared state.

After some ridiculous small talk about parking and traffic, he said, "Well, you haven't fled."

"No," I said. Honestly, that hadn't seemed like one of the options. If nothing else, I was hoping to find out the rest of the story.

Which was: At age twenty-four, living with the middle school secretary and their kids, he had had a motorcycle accident on a patch of gravel a hundred yards from his own front door. Right before he went into surgery to see if there was any shred of hope for his spinal cord, the middle school secretary declared her eternal allegiance to him and proposed marriage.

Which was funny, because he had at the same moment come to the conclusion that this was as good a time as any to break up. He would probably be living in rehab centers for months, or even a year—perfect. Sometime later in the telling of this tale he let it slip to me that he had since received two additional marriage proposals. "I guess I haven't lost *all* my charms, heh heh heh. *Anyway . . .*"

Anyway, I was mad at him. While he insisted I wouldn't have agreed to meet him if I had known about his wheelchair, I felt I would have been more positively disposed if I hadn't been tricked. I don't know if I would have been able to get over *heh heh heh, anyway,* the brown teeth, and the soon-to-be-revealed chain-smoking, but at this point it was a clusterfuck, and not a good setup for me to explore my flexibility vis-à-vis the chair.

I didn't see Wheelchair Mike again, though e-mails and phone calls trailed off gradually. I took down my profile and quit online dating forever, for the second time.

2. the perfect gentleman

One night in March—actually, the day that would have been my twenty-fourth wedding anniversary if I were still married to Tony, and also Texas Independence Day— my friend Dudley took me to a party at an artist's loft near the train station. To my amazement, the place was awash in Texas flags. It was a Texas Independence Day party. When Dudley introduced me to our host and I tried to explain why I was so delighted, he claimed to already know that this was my wedding anniversary, since he was an avid fan of my books. I'm still not sure I believe this, but it definitely put me in a good mood.

At the long table of tortillas from San Antonio and hot sauces from Austin (be still my heart), a tall, straight-backed man with thick, silver-white hair, kind eyes, weathered skin, and a bolo tie began chatting with me. I chatted back for a while, then wandered away. The next morning, I realized that this man was a prospect. He liked me. He was checking me out. So, maybe he was a little older than me. Maybe he hadn't blasted my hormones into outer space. What was I looking for, another Doucher?

Repentant, I tracked him down through our mutual acquaintances and asked him to come and look at a construction project in my backyard, heh heh heh. *Anyway* . . . Let us call this mustachioed gentleman The Walrus, which became Jane's nickname for him.

The Walrus was a fine and interesting man from a blue-collar Irish background who joined the navy at eighteen and has worked building houses since. He was also a talented stained-glass artist and visionary artisan, a freethinker, an in-line skater, a rock hound, bird-watcher, and conservationist, and very close to his grown daughter. He drank gin in the summer and bourbon in the winter. He had a costume closet for parades and masquerades and such. Jane absolutely adored him; nostalgic for his daddy days, he had nothing but rapt attention and silly jokes for her, and often showed up with little gifts.

He was the perfect family friend, but he was looking for something more substantial than that. I tried hard to get my feelings in line and to overcome what I knew was a lack of chemistry. On our first two dates without Jane I was quite aggressive, and things went well enough that he probably assumed we were hunky-dory. But I was losing focus. I guess I *was* looking for another Doucher, but one who wasn't such a douche.

On our third date, he took me to a party of his old friends where I could tell everyone had been prepped that he was bringing a new sweetie. I nibbled the fresh mozzarella balls and felt like a schmuck.

He must have been surprised on our fourth date when I awkwardly announced over drinks at Bertha's Mussels that I just wanted to be friends. I wasn't ready for the romantic part of romance. It's not you, it's me, blah blah blah. He took this sudden brush-off with equilibrium and said he would be happy to be my friend. And he has been my friend, though Jane would tell you we don't see him enough anymore. He showed up and sat at our table at a sock monkey workshop at the Visionary Art Museum last winter, and he made Jane a sock walrus.

I felt badly about this relationship. Meeting perfectly wonderful guys and treating them badly is not much less hellish than meeting jerks and getting dicked around. The Walrus deserved better.

3. the boy toy

While I was seeing The Walrus, Crispin went to Finland to address a philosophy conference and took his girlfriend. He and his girlfriend had been traveling a lot, to Walden Pond and to bluegrass festivals and other places I would have rather have cut off my foot than visit. It's good he's found a woman who lets him drive, I thought. A helpmeet, a sidekick, a muse: all roles pretty much out of my repertoire. This girlfriend was so different from me—not, thank God, a younger, cuter Marion Winik short-listed for the PEN/Faulkner—that I was starting to make my peace with the idea of her. She worked with special-needs children, she volunteered at the zoo; obviously, you can't hate such a person.

But I had not made my peace with single living, and I was still looking for biochemical fireworks. Around this time I ran into Zach Silverman, a thirty-something ex-student of mine on whom I had developed a secret crush. Zach Silverman had a beautiful girlfriend he was crazy about, but things were not working out for them at the moment. I knew a great deal about it because one of my primary conversation topics with Zach was his love life, about which I'd asked many sympathetic questions in the timeless tradition of the covetous counselor. We also talked a lot about spirituality, which he was pretty interested in even though he'd moved away from his Orthodox background.

Back when Silverman was my student, I tried not to focus on my crush, which arose from his cool art, his big brain, and his weirdly sexy, uptight, nineteenth-century Talmudic look. Obviously it was not a good idea. But at this point, he was not my student, and I started running into him around town more and more, possibly due to my sudden increased attendance at the avant-garde art openings and other events where Zach and his posse were found.

In the early summer of 2010, I became a habitué of postmodern Frisbee tournaments and video festivals, taking too much time to decide what to wear to them and drinking Natty Boh like a pro. Zach was always pleasant to me, but since our former professor-student relationship seemed to dictate this, I could never tell if he was aware of my crush, and if so, how he felt about it. Then one night after a show, I found Zach outside the club and bummed a cigarette from him (I bummed about a carton of cigarettes from him over the course of this thing; I should probably send him a check), smoking it while preening about and probably emitting a visible cloud of estrogen.

"Put away those shoulders," he said, both rudely and charmingly, since I do consider my shoulders one of my foremost assets.

At the end of the night he offered me a ride home; I was probably looking a bit unsteady. But I knew if I got in that car with him, all bets were off, so I refused and tottered along down the sidewalk.

Sometime in late June I was out with a single girlfriend of mine looking for something to do. Already a little tipsy, I texted Zach; he was at an MP3 release party at a place called The Taint, in a factory in a distant part of town. He said we should come on over but warned me that he was already very, very drunk. (Oh, no!)

We came upon the factory just before we would have been forced to go into a convenience store and ask if they could help us find The Taint, obviously the intention of the person who had named the place. ("Well, dear, it's right between the scrotum and the asshole!") We were halfway up the steps when my friend was abducted by pot-smokers in hats. As soon as I entered the party, Zach lurched toward me with a six of Natty Boh dangling from his index finger and asked me if I wanted to go look at the river.

He led me to a floodlit, garbage-swept concrete parking lot surrounded by a chain-link fence. I never saw any river; instead, with no further preliminaries, a furious make-out session was in progress. It was fun, but Zach and I had different ideas of what came next. I wanted to discuss our relationship; he wanted me to give him a blow job. This seemed beneath my dignity as a fifty-two-year-old mother of three, so I regretfully declined and we went back inside. He seemed to be about one millimeter away from either puking or alcohol poisoning, but was still on his feet when my friend and I left.

The next day my dignity went into remission and I e-mailed him to ask if he was having regrets, and if he wasn't, would he like to continue where we left off.

He reminded me of his incredible love for his girlfriend, and his desire not to repeat mistakes that had driven them apart in the past.

What could I say? I commended him. And I really do.

4. rock hudson

While smarting from the Silverman debacle, I received a friendly missive on Facebook from a gay guy I have known since high school, Ken, now living in New York. I already had a gay Ken in my life who was a little piqued by this latecomer, particularly when my new gay boyfriend and I began to refer to *him* as the Other Ken, or the O.K.

"What do you mean?! *He's* the Other Ken, not me!" Baltimore Ken said. He had a point; it was never settled.

Once a noted chef, a high-profile AIDS activist, and the hottest guy in the room, Manhattan Ken was running a little low on mystic powers. The erstwhile Pheromone King was struggling to live with HIV, hepatitis C, human papilloma virus, Meniere's disease, hepatic encephalopathy, and the wildest case of hypervigilance I have ever seen, probably due to PTSD from burying so many friends and clients since the 1980s. He was also in the thick of a multiyear attempt to get off benzodiazepines (Valium-type drugs), a withdrawal which causes horrible side effects, among which was the fact that he was only awake from the hours of eleven-thirty at night to three in the morning.

Night after night I set my alarm to wake up at this time and listen to him tell me about all the bacteria he had wrangled that day. As he went on and on, I sexted him a picture of me lying on the couch in my bikini underpants. My pent-up desires had apparently driven me around the bend. I'd been around it before. Raindrops on roses, whiskers on kittens, super-hot gay guys: my favorite things!

Finally, I stopped in to see him when I was visiting Hayes in New York. I found him living with two roommates in a spectacular two-bedroom penthouse apartment filled with sock monkeys. Yes, again with the sock monkeys; I don't know why they started appearing everywhere. If this was a novel, there would be some deeper meaning to it, but this is real life.

The Pheromone King was not explicit about the romantic arrangements of the household, but between the ratio of beds to people and the slightly weird vibes I received from his roommates, I came to my senses. And guess what, we are still friends. We are all friends, even the O.K., on Facebook.

Meanwhile, Vince had come home from New Orleans for the summer to try to make the money to pay me back for the fines and lawyer's fees relating to a recent Mardi Gras mishap. He couldn't find a job, so The Walrus took him on as a construction assistant. Oh Walrus, you are the man and I am a dickbag.

That's only four, I know. One more, the last one, is on the way.

the boomer
and the boomerang

Once he'd graduated from Georgetown with a degree in finance, Hayes was offered a six-figure salary in New York City at one of the big banks. I was amazed. In 1978, when I graduated from Brown with a degree in Russian history, I could hardly bring down four figures at the 7-Eleven.

Off he went to Manhattan, but it was no Summer of Love for him there. His girlfriend, the beauteous Queen of Ecuador (she was from an important South American family and looked like Penelope Cruz), dumped him two days after he got there. Meanwhile, the six-week training program at the bank was mind-numbingly dull. And while he had not liked New York when he'd lived there as an intern during the summer of his junior year, this time, he really hated it. Just making his way from his apartment to the subway in the sweaty morning rush-hour crowd was almost more than he could take.

My unflappable son began having what looked like a mini nervous breakdown. There were daily phone calls, there was crying, both unprecedented enough to warrant an impromptu visit. I offered names of therapists, prescriptions for Xanax and Zoloft, a $16 bowl of New York guacamole, and a pitcher of margaritas—I would have tried anything. I knew that Hayes was at an age where some young men develop schizophrenia, bipolarity, or a major depressive disorder. I have a cousin, now sixty, who has been institutionalized on and off since he graduated from Oberlin. So, actually, I was scared to death.

Not counting the death of his father when he was six, Hayes had had a pretty smooth ride to this point. In fact, a beleaguered, trouble-magnet high school friend of his had once joked that the entire Southern School District faculty and administration woke up each morning, scratching their heads and asking themselves, "What can I do for Hayes Winik today?" But now the proud HMS *Hayes* had sailed into the shallows.

One late summer night before Vince went back to college in New Orleans, he barged into my bedroom at 3:00 a.m., waving his cell phone. "You talk to him," he said. "He's a pussy!" Having grown up in the shadow of

Mr. Perfect / Ivan the Terrible, he had no idea how to deal with this weepy, crumbling incarnation of his life-long idol and oppressor.

The next week, Hayes took a leave from the bank, came home to Baltimore, and got not one but two jobs downtown. Apparently people were still wondering what they could do for Hayes Winik. He sublet his room in the Manhattan apartment we had just found, gave notice at work, stuffed his stuff back into my little Yaris, and had taken over my guest room by Labor Day.

I believe it's supposed to be a bad thing when your children end up back in the house after college, a sign of hard economic times and indulgent child-rearing prac-tices. Well, maybe older couples who have just finished saving for their long-postponed second honeymoon feel this way. Not me. While I was worried about Hayes's well-being, my nest was far from crowded, and there was no honeymoon activity in sight. Jane and I rejoiced at the return of her big brother.

As the leftovers in my fridge disappeared and my cabinets filled with giant urns of protein powder, as the pundits of ESPN *SportsCenter* returned to sing their lul-laby to the sleeping boy under the afghan on the couch, my heart was glad. Perhaps everything would be fine.

I had not really lived with Hayes since he'd graduated from high school in 2006, and that was hardly an idyllic time. We were in a farmhouse in rural Pennsylvania, my marriage to his stepfather was loudly and appallingly falling apart, and as any teenager would, Hayes judged me for the mess I had gotten myself into. *He* certainly wouldn't make mistakes like that because *he* was a much more sensible person than his crazy mother. Just as I had once figured out who I wanted to be by trying to be nothing like my mother, he had formed his identity in opposition to mine. Here is the simple version:

> My mother: Golfing, bridge-playing, stock-market-investing Yankees fan.
> Me: Bohemian, tattooed, poetry-writing Deadhead.
> My son: Golfing, high-school-football-playing, finance-majoring Cowboys fan.

If he looked down on me as an old hippie with weird friends, I had beefs about him as well. Most of them stemmed from what appeared to be his genuine belief that he could be in any number of places at once, and that all routine travel occurred at the speed of light. This is why, for example, he was in Atlantic City with my car when I landed at Baltimore/Washington International Airport, expecting him to pick me up. Ask his friends, ask his ex-girlfriend—we had all suffered. His charm usually got him out of any fixes he got himself into; as I mentioned earlier, even his therapist fell in love with him.

But post-breakup and breakdown, Hayes had apparently decided to be different. In addition to cutting most of the bullshit, he had mysteriously become a voracious reader, and was having me haul piles of nonfiction books and novels home from the library. *One Hundred Years of Solitude*. Teddy Roosevelt's autobiography. *Zeitoun*. He even read *Portnoy's Complaint*, my favorite novel. I had never seen such a thing.

More characteristically of young men in his age group, Hayes discovered the Paleolithic diet, which involved living the way the cavemen did, eating only the finest organic grass-fed beef and heirloom vegetables, and engaging in endless, mindless hours of physical exercise. Having finished unloading his wallet at Whole Foods, Paleolithic Man went to the gym, where he was known to dead-lift 400 pounds, after which he indulged in the protein shakes of the Iron Age. Paleolithic Man did not eat pasta, he did not drink lattes, and he was very suspicious of the ingredients his mother put in her supposedly carb-free casserole. Late in the Paleolithic era the discovery of vodka allowed these awesome, disease- and body-fat-free creatures to make vast advances in their ability to hunt and gather women.

I don't know if it was the diet, the literature, or the healing dose of family living, but Hayes's spirits were restored in a couple of months.

brown lips

That same fall, my food-writer friend Martha said she had a guy she wanted me to meet. Matt was smart and well-read, and he was a carpenter, a combination she thought would interest me. On the other hand, she warned, she did have a few concerns. He might not be over his last girlfriend, Foamy. (Fluffy? Sparky? Something like that.) The evidence of his broken heart was that he had drunk most of two bottles of wine, a tumbler of bourbon, and a martini the night Martha met him.

Well, I thought, send him on! Having been married to both a pain-pill addict and an alcoholic, neither of whom I was any help to at all, I could pretty much guarantee he'd end up in rehab.

However, Martha seemed unwilling to let us loose with each other's phone numbers, so instead, she decided to have a potluck dinner party to which we'd both be invited, along with other people, to take off the pressure.

This sounded like a good plan, weary as I was at this point of awkward getting-to-know-you conversations at the coffee shop.

Though I had somehow managed to spend the first fifty years of my life without going on a blind date, I now knew much more than I'd ever hoped to know about tedious first encounters. Still, I had not given up on the idea of finding love in any way possible. This time, like every other time, could be It. As usual, I threw myself into a delusional yet absorbing series of preparations.

Maybe my potluck dish for Martha's party was not the most important thing to worry about, but it was the most captivating for me. I welcome any chance to think about food for hours on end. I found a delicious-sounding recipe in the *Times* for something called a *panade*, involving layers of bread, chard, butternut squash, leeks, and cauliflower, baked with milk and Fontina cheese. While making my grocery list, I began to wonder if, along with the greens and grains, I might also need high-heeled leather boots and a pair of skinny jeans. In fact, I saw in a sudden flash of insight, it was the lack of these things that had been the roadblock to my dating success so far. I went straight to a resale shop to remedy the situation.

When I got home with my purchases, Hayes regarded me with amusement and doubt in his brown eyes. "Mom, these are Seven jeans," he said. "I know you didn't buy Seven jeans. They cost, like, $200."

Well, he would know, having inherited the shopping gene along with the brown eyes from his father, who by the way had had every excuse for pill-popping in the years before his death at thirty-seven. With tragedies like this in one's past, and God knows what on the agenda, one learns to enjoy every portent of a benevolent universe, no matter how small. The Miracle of the $28 Seven Jeans. Perhaps the start of a whole new run of luck!

When I got to Martha's that night, she revealed that she'd invited a second guy for me to check out, William. She'd met William on Match.com before she found Dan, and they had maintained a collegial friendship, since he was a writer.

"Oh, that dude," I said unenthusiastically. She had shown me a picture of him months earlier. "I thought he went to the West Coast or something."

"He did," she said. "But he's back."

As it turned out, William was somewhat more attractive in person than in his website photo—tall, fit, and clear-skinned, sort of bouncy and healthy-looking in a California-y way. The other guy, the brainy carpenter, had a more-grungy, six-days-on-the road thing going. Both of them paid a lot of attention to me throughout the evening, tag-teaming the seat next to me on the porch and vying for the chance to bring me a cocktail.

William told me all about his unpublished novel, which followed the spiritual quest of a young female character modeled on his twenty-two-year-old daughter. Fortunately, I was not quite so high on life that I agreed to read it. William seemed too New Age-y for me, but when I said this, he took it mildly. His consensus-building conversational style was a great relief, as I was still in recovery from the ten years of debate-club-on-steroids that was my second marriage.

Matt was also very nice, though a little less perky. He chugged whiskey, rolled his own cigarettes, blazed a few doobs on the balcony, but, you know, not necessarily in a suicidal way. He was actually rather courtly and sweet. I told him I had heard he'd been drowning his sorrows of late, and he smiled ruefully and asked me if I wanted to join him in a nightcap. Like William, he had a quality that made him so *not* my ex-husband, which in his case was the affectionate embrace of a panoply of vices and an aura of nonjudgmental, relaxed standards. After the sometimes ascetic, sometimes alcoholic, obsessive-compulsive Puritan philosopher I'd been married to, a nice, run-down enabler could be just what I needed. However, I didn't hear from him for quite a while.

Just two days later, I received a message from William. I considered whether to see him again. He wasn't that bad-looking, he was easy to talk to, and reasonably intelligent. As long as I could avoid his novel, I felt I had nothing to lose.

I had picked up his message on my iPhone as I was driving to hot yoga one morning. Just after that, I caught part of something interesting on the radio. It was an interview with actor Charles Dutton, who was coming to town with his one-man show, titled *From Jail to Yale*. It was at Morgan State University, a historically black college a couple miles up the road from me. It would be cool to see a play there, and, fortuitously, the event was on a Saturday, the night my daughter Jane regularly went up to stay over with her father in Pennsylvania.

William told me that he'd like to go to the show, but he'd have to order the cheapest tickets available because finances were an issue. Thinking ahead, I downloaded a coupon for dinner at a nice place over near the college.

When William got to my house that evening, I poured myself a glass of wine and prevailed upon him to join me. He was an unenthusiastic drinker, saying he'd never enjoyed a glass of wine before the other night at Martha's, when we'd opened several good bottles. "Sadly," he continued in his calm California way, "I'm fifty-four years old and find myself homeless, jobless, and penniless."

"Really?" I said. "How terrible for you!" It wasn't great for me either, at least in the short term. I slipped my restaurant coupon under a pile of newspapers and pulled out Tupperware containers of leftovers from the fridge.

William dug right into the chicken parmesan and continued. All the business ventures and freelance gigs he'd had going out West had tanked with the economy in the last year. When he ran out of options and rent money, he'd moved back home to Randallstown, a run-down suburban outpost of Baltimore, to stay on his mother's pullout couch. She was a Holocaust survivor, he said, who was already taking care of his sister, a morbidly obese young woman awaiting gastric bypass surgery, and her boyfriend, a crystal meth dealer.

"Jeez," I said, "how is your mother handling all this?"

"Well," he said thoughtfully, "the Holocaust, you know—it kind of puts things in perspective for her. I think she's just happy to have her family around."

Soon we were off to the show at Morgan State, where the "Will Call" line was so long and slow-moving that I wondered if we'd get to our seats before intermission. It seemed that every single African-American person in the city of Baltimore had come to this event. There are two thousand seats in the Morgan State auditorium, and no more than six of them were occupied by white people that night.

Under the fluorescent beams lighting the sidewalk where we waited, I studied my extremely white date out of the corner of my eye. His clothes, his salt-and-pepper hair, his smallish eyes. I hadn't noticed it before, but William's lips were unusual. They had a classic Cupid's-bow shape, but were very wide—like a three-quarter-inch lower lip—and very deeply colored. In fact, they were a sort of plummy brown. But really, more brown than plum.

"What's wrong?" asked William. "What are you looking at?"

"Oh, nothing," I said.

We finally got to our seats, which were on a precipitous fourth mezzanine perched at a dizzying height. We were surprised to see that Dutton had already begun his monologue, though many people had not yet gotten into the auditorium. I was annoyed to have missed the beginning of the story, since I had missed it on the radio, too, and the rest was pretty much word for word what I had already heard. Then Dutton announced that the remainder of the evening would consist of his doing scenes from Shakespeare with students from the Morgan State drama department.

William looked at me askance. "I had no idea," I whispered.

Without offering a single bit of background—you know, *This is a play about a bitter, insane old king who has three daughters*—Dutton launched into a medley of scenes from *King Lear*. A procession of young actors in Elizabethan costume swept onto and off the stage, shouting at each other in Old English, dueling, weeping, murdering, then carrying each other's dead bodies around and weeping some more. There seemed to be no end in sight.

Despite the mayhem onstage, soon our entire mezzanine looked as if sleeping gas had been released into the ventilation system. People collapsed over the arms and backs of their chairs, jaws dangling. Some sank into the pillowy bosom or muscled shoulder beside them; others remained nearly erect, nodding as discreetly as junkies in a driver's ed class.

Unbelievably, once finished with *Lear*, Dutton and his troupe moved on to *Richard III*.

Waking and stretching when awoken by the applause, which was thunderous once it became clear that the evening was truly over, my date gave me a sleepy smile. I felt guilty for having made him spend $35 on these tickets, and said so.

"Oh, it's fine," he said. "It's been a memorable experience, anyway."

We made our way to his car. I assumed we'd go out for a drink after the show, so was surprised when he rubbed his hands together and said, "God, I could really use some ice cream about now!"

"Ice cream?" I said. I started racking my brain for a place that served both ice cream and alcohol, which I felt I needed as soon as possible. "How about Golden West?" I suggested. "You can have a sundae and I can have a drink."

"Oh, I'd like to just go back to your place and chill," he said.

Fortunately it was dark in the car so he couldn't see the eye-rolling. "Actually, I don't have much ice cream," I said. "There's, like, one old ice-cream sandwich of Jane's." I explained that the sandwich in question was Birthday Party flavor, which meant it had pastel-colored nuggets in it, and that it had once been melted and refrozen and was now freezer-burned, but I was unable to dampen William's enthusiasm.

And because I am such a lame-ass pushover, home we went, and chill we did. He had his ice-cream sandwich,

and I sat down across the room with a bottle of Chardonnay. He chose a spot on the couch, so I sat in an
armchair as far away as I could without actually entering
the backyard. He told me more about his desperate straits,
his fascinating relatives, and his romantic history. I talked
about my once-beautiful, intensely passionate marriage
and how it had been tragically destroyed by distrust, alcohol, and bitterness. Somehow I meandered from there to
the subject of my fantasy beach house. Since our mother's
death, my sister Nancy and I had been talking about buying a place in New Jersey so we could have a way to
get together in our old home state. William perked up at
this turn in the conversation and suggested that he could
move in and house-sit if we did.

Finding it hard to keep my mind on the discussion
at hand, I remembered suddenly that I hadn't seen any of
my road atlases since I'd moved to Baltimore, now going
on two years ago. Where were those road atlases? Though
I had not used a road atlas in a long time—in fact, I had
bought these as gifts for my sons back when they first got
their driver's licenses, and they had abandoned them when
they went off to college—earlier in the day I had wanted
to consult a real live paper map to see if there was any way
to get to the Jersey shore from Baltimore without taking 95 through Delaware, which has been backed up with

traffic for several decades. Whether it was ADD, OCD, or just conversational desperation, I was suddenly driven to jump up and look for these road atlases in my office.

He took this opportunity to put in a call to his mother, which I overheard as I pawed through a cabinet of gift wrap.

"No, Mom, just go to bed. Don't worry about pulling out the couch or anything. That's too much for you. Please. Just put a pillow and a blanket out for me and go to bed. I won't be home 'til three or four, anyway."

"Are you kidding?!" I shouted, fierce and hoarse as King Lear. "I have to go to bed in a half-hour."

William rolled with the punches and told his mother he'd be home by midnight; 11:30, I suggested. At 11:15, I yawned and said, "Okay, well. . . ." I really needed to get back to looking for those atlases.

He lifted his eyebrows and a smile curved his brown lips, which I had by now studied more thoroughly, with poor results. "Well," he said suavely, "before I go, how 'bout some touching?"

For a moment or two there was absolute silence, then I couldn't help it, I started laughing. He looked hurt. "Why are you laughing?" he asked plaintively.

Guilty and red-faced, I said, "Oh, I'm sorry, I—damn. What do you mean by touching?"

"Well," he said, "you sit next to me on the couch and I put my arm around you."

I plopped myself down a few inches away from him. He draped an arm around me, then began to massage my shoulder, then drew me closer to him. I leaned into his sweater, hoping this would be the end of it. But he put his other arm around me and attempted to move into a hug position, his hands now fervently grasping and rubbing my back. I could almost feel his blood pressure rise, his muscles tense, the throbbing pulse beneath that tranquil California facade, and I didn't even want to know what was going on in his pants. I leapt from the couch as if ejected from a cannon, and he apologized and apologized and somehow we got from there to the front door.

I never did locate those atlases. But after this evening, there was no longer any doubt that I was lost. I obviously had no idea how to be a single woman of a certain age, and I was about ready to give up on my approach so far. None of the men I had met in the preceding months was even a distant relative of The One. On the contrary, each had nudged me closer to waking up from my girlish dream. Realistically, the mating rituals of people in their twenties and thirties might *never* work for me at this point in life. Could I try something else now?

Through the pane in the front door, I watched William drive away down the street; actually, I made sure William *did* drive away down the street. I breathed a sigh of relief and turned away. There was a shifting in the rumpled nest of woolen blankets on the loveseat, the position from which my dachshund Beau monitored all comings and goings from the house. He poked his long, velvety nose out between the fringes of the afghan, an expectant look in his shining brown eyes. He'd known all along whom I would end up with in bed that night.

love in the time
of baltimore

Like a jalopy sputtering to a halt, I had my last few backfires.

"I'm not really dating anymore," I told Matt the carpenter when he called, but I met him for dinner in a Fells Point tavern anyway. "I have my friends," I told him earnestly, "my family. My work. I'm busy, I'm happy. I'm starting to think of being single as a way of life, not a state of emergency, an urgent problem that has to be solved."

Matt looked bemused. He told me many of the women in our age group he goes out with say the same thing. He thinks it's the men who are really driven to pair up again, while women can make do with what they have left over from their original families.

He wasn't the only person who told me this. One of the last guys I met for coffee, courtesy of an eleventh-hour, hope-springs-eternal online dating relapse, was a hatchet-faced cynic with the demeanor of a failed, embittered Catskills comedian. He listened to the beginning of my apologetic anti-dating speech, nodding sourly.

"Oh, let me guess," he interrupted. "You're very close to your children and your dog? And you have a warm, loving circle of friends? What a surprise!"

Of course now that I had really given up hope, romantic possibilities were coming out of the woodwork. Even my therapist, whom I had stopped seeing at her suggestion, tried to fix me up with a guy who turned out to be my friend Martha's ex-husband. A mom at the school took me clubbing with her Italian hairdresser, Fabrizio: cute, suave, brusque in a Corleone-family way; I don't think I was his type either. Our cursory attempt at fooling around at 3:00 a.m. was unsuccessful. Possibly he hadn't had time to take his Viagra. Also, he had shaved his back hair and it was growing back, which was not a good thing.

A radio traffic announcer I met during the online-dating relapse asked me to meet him for a drink. He weighed between three and four hundred pounds, but not for long, he explained. Since the heart attacks, his doctor had him on a strict diet.

A man from Germantown, Maryland, addressed me frantically as I tried to get off the phone with him: "But what will I do about my driving lust?"

Even Matt, though apprised of my anti-romance stance, was not giving up completely. After a fun night at Martha's fiftieth birthday party, he told me I was an "enchanting woman." Geez. Suddenly my appeal was such that I couldn't even walk into the Memphis airport without some born-again Christian defense contractor trying to buy me drinks.

One night, I had a serious craving for white clam pizza—a particular white clam pizza from a place called Pepe's in New Haven, Connecticut, was what I had in mind, but I'd had good luck re-creating it at home over the years. I thought about it day and night: how I would make the crust with a little cornmeal, where I would get the clams, whether I would stick with garlic, parsley, and red pepper, or recklessly add Parmesan. I thought about the pizza constantly, but I did not make it. Jane doesn't eat white clam pizza, and neither does Ken. Hayes was out of town. So . . . who would I make it for?

After about a week of thinking about that pizza, I decided I didn't need anybody else to serve it to. I made it just the way I'd been thinking of, too spicy for most people but perfect for me, and I sat down at my kitchen table and ate it all, with just a few bites slipped to the dachshund.

Single life would work just fine for me, I thought. Which was good, because my divorce was about to be final.

Though Crispin and I had been supposedly in the process of obtaining a divorce for about a year, there had been no rush as far as I was concerned. I had health insurance through his employer, and Vince was still receiving college tuition assistance. But Crispin had told me the preceding summer that his girlfriend's Catholic family had problems with her dating a married man, and it was time to get the show on the road. Our divorce should be simple—we owned nothing in common, had no disagreements about custody or money, and had been living apart for almost two years.

In August I went to court and testified to our irreconcilable differences. By late September, the decree was on its way. I wrote Crispin an e-mail wishing him well, explaining that the judge had warned each of us not to "hire a hall" until the final paperwork was in hand. To my surprise he replied immediately with this P. G. Wodehouse quote:

> His soul, as he walked, was a black turmoil of
> conflicting emotions. This woman had treated
> him in a way which would have made even a
> man with so low an opinion of the sex as the
> late Schopenhauer whistle incredulously. But
> though he scorned and loathed her, he was

annoyed to discover that he loved her still. He would have liked to bounce a brick on Prudence Whittaker's head, and yet, at the same time, he would have liked—rather better, as a matter of fact—to crush her to him and cover her face with burning kisses. The whole situation was very complex.

What the hell? The moment of divorce seemed a bizarre time to express such a sentiment. Or perhaps it was meant to be nostalgic; Crispin's love had always been exactly like a combination of bouncing bricks and burning kisses. In any case, after staring wide-eyed at my laptop screen for a few minutes, I decided to take it as a tribute to our past—I couldn't imagine what else to do.

Crispin's mother Joyce is one of the coolest people I know—a tiny, birdlike woman in her eighties with bright blue eyes and soft white hair, and more intellectual, moral, and social vigor than most people half her age. Or any age, really. When my own mom was alive, I used to look at the two of them—independent, intelligent, full of zest, and doing exactly what they wanted to all the time—and think, *When do I get to be an elderly widow?*

Every year in late fall, Joyce puts on an annual show—
a performance where she and other residents of her rural
Virginia area (many of whom are accomplished retirees
from Washington, D.C.) do dramatic monologues about
their lives. It is amazing how she can get everyone from
the county clerk to a local horse rancher to the former
ambassador to Nepal to do this, and she herself tells a
story every year.

Last year, I didn't go to Joyce's show. And I didn't
attend her birthday party or my stepdaughter Emma's
graduation either, largely because Crispin's girlfriend
the zoo volunteer went to all of these things. This year, I
decided I didn't care if the girlfriend went or not; I wasn't
going to miss the show. I made arrangements to stay with
one of Joyce's friends.

At the last minute, Joyce called with two pieces of
information: Her friend had broken her arm and couldn't
have a houseguest, and the girlfriend would not be coming down after all. "You'll just stay with me," Joyce
announced. Father and daughters would be up in the loft
and I would sleep with her, she said.

"Okay," I agreed. "If you think so."

So we caravanned down there, Crispin with Jane
and Emma, I with the dog, and it went smoothly, except
for a stop at the always-controversial Dinosaur Land gift

shop, full of cheap tchotchkes with a half-life of three days, so beloved by him and the children, so despised and eschewed by me. Once we were at the farm, Joyce surrounded me with her usual love and good vibes as I stood in the kitchen, making her favorite Thai chicken with coconut milk. From an armchair behind her, her son was sparkling at me, too.

I felt funny even being in the same room with him— we had not spent five minutes together in years. I kept thinking that he should have brought his girlfriend; if she wasn't a part of this new era of getting along, she would surely feel jealous and left out.

That night, after another glorious triumph for the storyteller-thespians of Rappahannock County, Crispin and the girls went up to bed and I crawled into bed with my ex-mother-in-law. We slept under an Amish quilt we had bought over a decade earlier for her and her husband Richard, who died in 2002. Exhausted from the day's events, I passed out in minutes.

In the early morning I was half-awake when I felt a little hand patting my shoulder. I opened my eyes and there was Joyce, lying in bed beside me, beaming.

"Life is so strange, isn't it, Marion?" she said.

Yes it was, and it was about to get a whole lot stranger.

✻ ✻

That morning after breakfast Joyce explained that some-one had to go back to the theater where the performance had been held and put away the chairs and risers. With-out thinking much about it, I said to Crispin, "Come on, we'll go. Let the girls get some time with your mom."

Really? everyone thought, including me. These two are going to get in a car and go do an errand together? Hope it goes all right.

It did. We chatted about this and that as we worked, hurrying through the awkward situation even as it was turning out to be not so bad. Finally I said, "So why didn't you bring your girlfriend?"

"She wanted to come," he said. "But I didn't think I could handle it. Her, you, my mother, Emma, all in one little room. . . ."

"Yes, but in the future you have to bring her," I urged. "It's the only way it'll be all right for me to be included in stuff like this."

He didn't say any more.

A few minutes later we left the church, but both of us paused on the threshold, unwilling to leave this moment behind. Without looking at him I blurted, "Do you ever think about how sad it is that we completely destroyed that beautiful love we had?"

"Of course I do," he said, and when I turned and looked in his eyes, I saw not nostalgia but regret and anger and pain. He looked at his watch. "We should go," he said hoarsely. We jumped in the car and headed back to his mom's.

About a week later, he sent me an e-mail saying he'd thought at first he wouldn't tell me, but in fact he had just broken up with his girlfriend. Before I had any intellectual reaction to this news, I felt the blood drain out of my upper body.

It turned out that our divorce, though intended to facilitate their moving in together, buying a house, and getting engaged, had ended up having the opposite effect. Apparently he had been trying to wriggle out of the situation for several months, and now, faced with the reality of having become fully available, he had called it quits.

About a week after that I received an e-mail from him announcing that he loved me but he could never be with me again. It went on from there. "I think if we did try again it would consist of, you know, twelve hours of ecstasy, twelve of agony, and then right back to as profound as possible a separation, where I'd be working for months to find the sort of detachment I have now, however much that actually is. Meanwhile, your self-esteem would peak at hour six, and crash inexorably at hour sixteen, leaving you with the necessity of more therapy! It's just not a promising direction."

I was not arguing. He was coming at me with that mixture of bricks and kisses that I knew so well—and had spent so much time recovering from, sitting in my Georgian airplane hangar, playing Stevie Nicks's "Landslide" over and over on the guitar. I had put all that behind me now.

Except maybe I hadn't. Maybe inside me there was still a raging river of affection and attraction looking for a hole in the dike. Without actually deciding to do it, I found myself being a whole lot nicer to him.

One weekend when I came to drop off Jane, I brought groceries to Crispin's little hobbit house in the woods and cooked dinner there. The three of us spent a sweet evening together and Jane was glowing. When I left, Crispin followed me out to my car and tenderly kissed me good-bye. His hands were on my waist, his thumb pressing lightly into a spot near my hipbone that tingled for hours afterwards. All the hard work I had put into trying to forget the intensity of our physical connection crumbled in the face of that thumbprint.

Afterwards, he told me later, he had apparently been staring goofily into space. "What are you thinking about, Daddy?" asked Jane.

"Oh, nothing," he replied.

"I know what it is," she said.

"What?"

"You're thinking about Mommy."

Now the e-mails really kicked into high gear. On January 11, four days before Jane and I left for a ten-day visit to Judy and Lou, who had moved from D.C. to France, Crispin came to my house a few hours before he went to school to pick up Jane for their Wednesday-afternoon visit.

It was like the first time, it was like the last time, it was what I had been living so gracelessly without, physically ecstatic and emotionally explosive. I was helpless before the primacy of my body and its urges and chemicals, which were smoothing the rough edges of this situation with an endorphin blaze that almost completely blocked rational thought. By the time we went downstairs and I began to sauté mushrooms for an omelet, I had an idiotic smile on my face that wouldn't quit, and I could hardly put two words together to form a sentence.

Which was good because we decided to keep our "reconciliation" (or whatever it was) a secret. There were many reasons for this. It was likely that people who had seen what Crispin and I did to each other in the first decade of this millennium would receive news of our reunion with about the same credibility afforded your average Holocaust denier. Among these potential naysayers were both of our oldest children, Emma and Hayes, who were particularly protective of each of us.

Emma, whom I had for better or worse always treated more as a friend than as a daughter, had heard my "snow goose" rap. These birds are biologically driven to mate for life, sometimes as long as thirty years. I had felt since the day I met her father that despite the big and small incompatibilities between us—Apollonian loner / Dionysian extrovert—there was an interlock between us deeper than rhyme or reason. When I told myself in the last years of our marriage that we should stay together even though we were destroying each other, it was largely because I believed this. But Emma had seen it differently. She did not want to see her father drink himself to death as he nearly had back then, when she had felt so powerless, and she was pretty sure I wasn't helping. Would things be different now? He had stopped drinking almost the very day he'd left me. Could he come back without stumbling?

Hayes, too, had never recovered from the tensions of the last days and the terrible meltdown at the end. Since he was still living with me for another month, I was particularly anxious about his reaction. He had briefly encountered his former stepfather a few times since he'd moved home, while helping me drop off or retrieve Jane. He had behaved cordially yet coolly, and I was pretty sure this was as far as he was interested in going.

I did tell Sandye almost immediately, my voice dreamy with happy brain chemicals. She said, Oh my. She hadn't seen it coming but was not completely surprised, and warned me to be careful. I also told my friend Judy, too, a few days after Jane and I got to her house in France during winter break. She, too, said to be careful.

I didn't need to be told. I *was* being extremely careful, and my emotions did not defrost as fast as my body did. Through the early months of the rapprochement, each advance in closeness was followed by a backlash, usually in the form of an unexpectedly critical or chilly e-mail from Crispin. At first, we were unthinkingly drawn into our old ways, our harsh, obsessive, five-e-mails-per-hour arguments, and several times it seemed we would quickly go off the rails. But there was no point in this, and we knew it. So we'd just let it go, retreat to our separate lives, and cool off.

In March, we told Jane we were dating, as if she needed to be told, and then we told everyone else. People were shocked, people were moved, some were kind of pissed, and just about every single one said "Be careful." Hayes was more in the pissed group, but fortunately he had just moved out. He and a couple friends from high school had found a place three blocks from the Federal Hill party district and proceeded to unleash themselves on the bar scene. Paleolithic Man reminded me a lot of High School Man, except with more money.

Joyce clipped an advice column from the *Washington Post* on Valentine's Day and sent it to me. "*Dear Amy,*" read one of the letters, all from long-term couples who did not cohabit. "*My husband and I have lived separately for 20 years because of financial/employment circumstances. We attribute our enduring marriage to this arrangement, since we are a somewhat mismatched couple.*"

Well, we were definitely in that category with her. So, it seemed, were others in my age group. "In the 40s and beyond, many women have that 'been there, done that' feeling, and are craving a different lifestyle option," explained a Dr. Deb Castaldo in an article I ran into online. "The rules of the monogamy game have changed drastically. Many women are now consciously redefining exclusive relationships that are emotional, sexual, committed, and, best of all, part-time. This new way of dating is not driven by rigid moral expectations of traditional marriage, [but] rather by individual needs for both intimacy and independence."

So would Crispin and I end up in adjoining condos in the senior apartment complex? My friend Therese didn't seem to think so. Having witnessed our dark days, she was shocked at first by the news of our accord. Then she told me she'd noticed that often couples with very brutal, hateful divorces would end up back in each other's arms after a cooling-off period—not because they had really solved their problems and were getting back together, but because they had had enough time and space to remember what had brought them together in the first place (yes, the sex, but not *just* the sex). After a certain interval of kindness and connection, they would drift apart, this time leaving things in a better place.

I was quiet when she said this, not sure she was wrong. Our incompatibilities and distrust and emotional crimes against each other were very real, and we bumped up against them more frequently as we tried to be boyfriend and girlfriend. Attempting to navigate around the danger zones was turning us into something more like friends with benefits than lovers.

Then I started to lose interest in the benefits. Which was not like me at all, especially considering the fireworks that had occurred when the benefits first returned. But by the summer of 2011, I was feeling other things I had never felt before. I was so tired sometimes, crazy tired. I didn't know if it was age, perimenopause, or low-grade depression, or maybe I was just turning lazy, but twice I had to leave my hot yoga class halfway through, which was unheard-of for me. Sometimes the exhaustion came so abruptly that I felt knocked to the couch, the lights in my head going out with a dizzy whoosh.

Not so long ago, I had considered taking a nap almost humiliating. Naps were for pussies. Something was definitely going on.

the decline and fall
of the party people

I am the opposite of those people who won't take a sip from your glass or kiss you when you have a cold, who festoon the toilet seat with whorls of paper. I like to say I don't believe in the germ theory of disease transmission, and if that's not exactly true, I do believe that an ounce of prevention is not much better than an ounce of dirt. Once I heard part of a radio interview with a 107-year-old Russian woman who attributed her longevity to never peeling her vegetables, eating yogurt, and drinking vodka. She could have been my guru.

I was the Impervious One. I never missed a day of school or work due to illness. I had tramped through Mexico with friends dropping left and right from *turista* and had nary a cramp. I never got the flu, rarely caught a cold, escaped herpes and AIDS—especially noteworthy since I was married to someone who died of it. My sister also failed to get AIDS in a similar situation, adding to my impression that I was from a race of half-Russian demigods.

Not long after Tony died I went in for an annual checkup, and the blood work showed that my liver enzymes were elevated. This could have been because I'd had a few glasses of wine the night before, but further testing showed that I had antibodies to hepatitis C.

A lot of people have hepatitis C—4 million in the United States, 170 million worldwide. Many of them don't even know they have it because they have no symptoms. You can be symptom-free for decades, or for life. On the other hand, you can develop liver scarring, which leads to cirrhosis, which can cause liver cancer or just kill you all on its own.

How did so many people get hepatitis C? While about half of those diagnosed have a history of injecting drugs, and transfusion was a possibility before they started screening the blood supply in 1992, many people can't figure out how they could have contracted it. Getting a tattoo or piercing, sharing a razor or toothbrush, and snorting drugs (blood can get on the straw) are all possibilities.

Anyway, I was not in the Don't Know group. I knew, all right. When I didn't get AIDS, I got this. Every demigod has that spot on his heel.

No big deal; I wasn't worried about it. I had no symptoms, and a biopsy showed that my liver was fine. I also didn't worry about infecting other people, as heterosexual transmission is rare to nonexistent, and I was no longer partying with syringes or rolled-up dollar bills. These facts somewhat reassured Crispin during our ten years together, but every once in a while he would knit his brow and go in for a test. Each time it turned out that those faux pas with the toothbrush had left him unscathed.

In utero transmission was harder to dismiss, so when I got pregnant in 1999, I visited a gastroenterologist, the specialty that covers the liver. The risk was pretty low, it turned out, and my daughter Jane was born without the virus, as her older brothers Hayes and Vince had been.

Once a year I repeated the blood tests; every five years, a biopsy. Each time they saw me, though my condition hadn't changed, my doctor and his assistant urged me to get treatment—a form of chemotherapy that lasts from six months to a year. In the mid-2000s, the chance of cure was about fifty-fifty.

The interferon treatment was infamous for its side effects—depression, fatigue, and flu-like symptoms (whatever they might be; don't ask me, the Impervious One). One of my sister's husbands had relapsed on drugs and died in the middle of treatment. The husband who followed him, one of the most even-tempered and physically fit people I know, also had to treat for hepatitis C. He became cranky, quit going to the gym, and sometimes didn't make it into work. He was cured, though. Others I knew were not.

Should I inject toxic drugs that would make me feel bad and might not work, when I felt just fine? I thought not. Well, my physician reminded me, the catch-22 was that if I waited until I didn't feel fine, I would have less chance of a cure.

Maybe I should quit drinking alcohol, he went on. The recommended limit for those with hepatitis C is one drink per year. I found this extremely amusing.

The year I moved to Baltimore, I began to have occasional pains in my upper right abdomen. I remembered from experience with a boyfriend who was a heavy drinker of Bushmills Irish Whiskey (and often staggered around in the morning, clutching his right side) that this might be liver pain. I cut down my drinking, which dovetailed well with my rapprochement with Crispin. He had been sober since the day he'd moved out, and had very little interest in being around alcohol—still less in watching me drink it. Still, the pangs didn't stop. I made an appointment with a new doctor in Baltimore.

Not long after that, it began—the Summer of Pancytopenia and Splenomegaly. Tests showed that I had very low red and white blood counts (that's pancytopenia) and a spleen that was visibly and uncomfortably about three times the usual size (that's splenomegaly). This explained why I had become such a pussy lately, with the naps and all.

My doctor thought the changes in my condition were sudden enough that something else might be wrong besides hepatitis C. Two other liver doctors, a hematologist/oncologist and a surgeon, were enlisted to give their opinions. I had, over the next few months, two ultrasounds, a CT scan, an endoscopy, a colonoscopy, a bone marrow biopsy, a liver biopsy, a spleen biopsy, an MRI, and scores of blood tests, giving my new health insurance quite a workout.

We baby boomers like to do things in packs, so I was not too surprised when my problems turned out to be part of a trend. "We're starting to see a lot of people like you," said more than one of the doctors I visited. Many boomers had been walking around with hepatitis C since our salad days thirty years ago, and now many were starting to experience the first signs.

The Summer of Pancytopenia and Splenomegaly wasn't all bad. I enjoyed having smart, personable doctors pay so much attention to me, discuss me in conferences, ponder the mysteries of my condition, discuss whether I should have an operation to remove my now mini-fridge-size spleen. I was a fascinating puzzle! The oncologist, a motherly Chinese woman, laughed at my jokes. A young, good-looking infectious disease fellow at Hopkins was impressed that I was a writer. The doctors seemed to care about me and even answered my e-mails. When I answered the question "What brings you here today?," all agreed that I was an accomplished medical historian. I smiled. I was always good at using vocabulary words in a sentence.

I looked forward to my doctors' appointments and often dressed up for them, either in blue, to bring out my eyes, or in red, which I felt accentuated my health. It was sort of like getting ready for a date. Perhaps I was developing a strain of Munchausen syndrome, where people feign a disease because they enjoy the attention. Except I wasn't feigning. And though I liked going to doctors, I was testy about the interest in my condition elsewhere.

I had been famous for being the person who never had the flu. Now I had people talking behind my back about my spleen biopsy. I had been through a disorienting identity loss like this before, actually. Because I skipped a couple of grades in school, I spent the first several decades of my life as the youngest person in every situation. So precocious and cute, like Doogie Howser.

My Doogie days were over a long time ago. I was not the Young One anymore; I was the Old One. At this point I was the Old, Sick One.

When I started to experience actual ill health, I remembered Tony and my mother and other people whose last months on earth I had superintended while bouncing around like Jesus at the leper colony. Oh, *this* was fatigue. *This* was fever and chills. These were the infamous flu-like symptoms. At least, I thought, it was a course in empathy.

Most of the ways I thought about being sick—Munchausen syndrome, course in empathy, etc.—were ways of being detached from it, my own version of my mother's machismo. Sometimes, though, I did feel the fear. Usually I avoided speaking of it, but one day as I was leaving the examining room of the good-looking young infectious disease fellow, I stopped on the threshold.

"My father died when he was fifty-six," I said suddenly. "Three years older than I am now." My eyes filled with tears as I thought about how much younger my children were than I was then—my children that my father never saw—Hayes and Vince, who would be without a mother or a father, Jane so very young. There was no way to put all this into words.

The doctor returned my gaze with clear sympathy in his eyes. After a moment, he said simply, "I very much want you to have a positive outcome, and I believe you will."

That fall, my red blood count improved for reasons unknown, and I started to feel better. Meanwhile, the myriad tests had ruled out lymphoma, liver cancer, tuberculosis, and maybe things I never knew were on the list. I just had hepatitis C, and it had caused cirrhosis. The good news was that there are new drugs with fewer side effects and greater success, and they were in trials right here in Baltimore.

The bad news: It took me too long to smell the coffee, and my blood counts were too low to get into a trial. I would have to take the bad old drugs, and I would have to start soon. Probably I was not alone. Probably many other former badass demigods were somewhere out there canceling their gym memberships and pursuing new hobbies, like napping, drinking decaffeinated tea, and watching all seven seasons of *The Gilmore Girls* in a couple of months. Spending our days swallowing pills, driving to blood tests, getting product recommendations in previously unknown aisles of the drugstore.

Oh, guys. We are so busted.

In January, I spent a couple of hours getting trained in the regime I would be following in the year ahead. Syringes, biohazard-disposal cans, pill sorters, and electronic alarms were involved. The first three months I would be on Telaprevir, a very strong but extremely effective medication that had to be taken every eight hours with 20 grams of fat. (This upset me as much as anything else, imagining myself ballooning up like a force-fed duck on its way to becoming foie gras.) But if you didn't eat the fat, I was warned, the medicine couldn't be absorbed, and you would get something known as "burning butt" or "poop of fire."

There was a huge stack of printed materials from the drug manufacturers to inform me about potential side effects. As I shoved them back into the box, a treatise titled "Dealing with Itching" caught my eye. How much could there be to say? Meanwhile, the doctor explained that many of the side effects were cumulative, particularly depression, which set in for roughly half the patients. With whom did I live? she asked. This person might have to be the arbiter of whether I needed antidepressants—whether I was becoming progressively crankier.

Well, I wasn't sure. Should a person's eleven-year-old daughter really be in charge of this decision?

That afternoon I gave myself my first Interferon shot, took my first handful of pills, ate my first avocado, cream cheese, and smoked salmon bagel. It wasn't that bad. I was low on energy, headachy, a little feverish, but I'd been subpar for a year already, so it was no big shock. I took it in stride when a good friend presented me with a silver and turquoise Virgin Mary charm. A Miraculous Medal, she explained, representing Mary's power to heal those who believe.

As a Jewish atheist, I was not really one of them, but I clasped that thing on a silver chain around my neck in two seconds flat.

A couple days later, Jane came home with news of an epidemic of head lice in her class—of course, raking her nails through her hair as she spoke.

I blanched, knowing full well from experience with my older kids what an anti-lice campaign involved—like, ten times as much energy as I had.

"Oh my God," I said in a sepulchral tone. A few minutes later, when I asked her to put in her retainer, she said it might be in her lunchbox, and her lunchbox might be . . . in Ms. Lewis's classroom?

"Are you kidding me?" I screamed. I was already two $150 retainers into the orthodontic journey.

"Look!" she said accusingly, surveying my crumbling face. "It's happening already! You better call and get those pills."

Blood work taken two weeks after I started the drugs showed my viral load down from over three million to forty-three. Forty-frickin'-three. This was not an unusual result, but it was a very good one. I was almost cured.

So, I thought, this is what I was so afraid of all those years? This little nothing treatment? Miracle Mary loves Jewish atheists! Let the joyous phone calls begin!

The next afternoon, my right forearm began to feel sore. By the time I put Jane to bed, it had gotten quite serious. I didn't have a moment free from agony until I gave in at 5:00 a.m. and called Ken to take me to the emergency room.

By then, the arm was swollen, and reddish areas were spreading. I was diagnosed with cellulitis, a tissue infection. They gave me a little morphine, a little Dilaudid, then sent me home with an antibiotic. Perhaps the reckless scratching caused by Telaprevir, plus my dirty fingernails, plus my depressed immune system from the Interferon, had added up to mad, crazy bacteria having an orgy in my arm. No one else came up with any better ideas.

I guess I should have read "Dealing with Itching" more carefully.

The next five days were bad. My arm ended up double its normal size, bright red, and burning hot. Layers of dermis had peeled off so that it looked skinned in some places, and spotted with boils in others. My son Hayes gagged the first time he saw it. Meanwhile, the antibiotic was ravaging my digestive system. Soon I couldn't swallow and had something that felt like hydrochloric acid pouring out of my ass at ten-minute intervals. I had to take four of those pills every day and I shook with terror each time.

Many dear people in my neighborhood were taking care of me—bringing me food and beverages, doing my errands, wrapping me in gauze, driving Jane around—but, as my arm continued to putrefy, all were increasingly insistent that I should go back to the hospital. But it's the first week of classes! I told them. I can't miss school! I can't leave Jane! What about the dog? And finally: You are not the boss of me, Pam Stein!

But, in fact, I was not doing anything for Jane but scaring her, and I was so weak I had to teach my undergraduate class flat on my back from my sickbed, via Skype. Immediately following, poor abused Pam took me to the doctor and then on to Johns Hopkins Hospital. The antibiotic was not the right one after all, and the infection was out of control.

Crispin, who had been very sweet and concerned about me since my health troubles started, took time off from work to come down and stay with Jane and Beau. By now our transition to friends without benefits was well established, and we rarely had a cross word. However, living in my house while I was hospitalized reminded him of annoying things about me he had escaped from when our domestic union dissolved, so we did share some nostalgic moments of snarkery.

For example, back in the day he had chafed under my hated regime of reusing plastic grocery bags to line my garbage can instead of purchasing real (and much roomier) kitchen trash bags. I had no Glad, and this made him sad. Having escaped from this nightmare three years earlier, and stocking his cabinets with every size, thickness, and closing style of plastic bag possible, he had forgotten about my stupid system. But now, shortly after I'd been admitted to Johns Hopkins, he found himself ransacking my house to find my trash bags. He called me in my hospital bed at about 7:30 am.

"Where are your trash bags?" he demanded.

"My trash bags?" I said. "Are you kidding? Isn't this why we got divorced?" We started sputtering at each other immediately.

"Your garbage is overflowing!" he accused me.

"That's not the bag's fault!" I retorted. "That's because you didn't take it out!"

Only the sudden beeping of my IV line put a stop to it.

Trash bags, thermostats, and other technical difficulties aside, he was a lifesaver.

After fighting so hard not to go there, I loved the hospital. The first object of my affection was my nurse Geri, a big, kind African-American woman who tried to speed the process for me as I waited for the phlebotomist to show up and draw the blood required before I could start medication. Soon enough, I was falling apart.

"Can't you just do it yourself?" I pleaded with the resident on the floor after about six hours. "You're a doctor, right?" As she demurred—this was a complicated blood draw—Geri broke in and said, "I can do it."

That is just the beginning of what she did. She fixed everything, took care of everything, constantly soothed me with endearments and reassurances. After what I'd been through at home, I felt like I was at a spa.

At night, Geri was replaced by the awesome Lucky—a spiky blonde with horn-rimmed glasses who had three months' nursing experience to Geri's decades'. Eventually I found out she had been a policy analyst in Washington until the corruption drove her out of there, screaming. She started nursing school at age forty.

Lucky and Geri and I were bonded not only by their care for me, but by our shared project: my extraordinary roommate, Miss Simpson.

Miss Simpson, a bone-thin African-American woman who sometimes looked like a twelve-year-old boy, and sometimes like a ninety-year-old crone, was very, very unhappy about being in the hospital, though she was rushed in with a fever of 105 degrees the same day as me. When anyone came to take her vitals or bring her meds, she screamed with fury. GET AWAY FROM ME. I DON'T WANT THAT! Our room was in an uproar around the clock, partly because she wouldn't (or couldn't) use her call button when her empty IV beeped, or when she needed to go to the bathroom.

This was the beginning of our friendship.

"Do you want me to call the nurse for you, Miss Simpson?" Amazingly, over the course of three days, we got to the point where I could crack jokes about her stubbornness.

"I like Marion," Miss Simpson announced one day, though she had never opened the curtain between our beds. "Where's Marion? What's Marion having for lunch? Why didn't I get that? I want what Marion has!" Lucky said it was like a darn sorority in there.

What impressed me most was the commitment to taking care of her. Miss Simpson refused a spinal tap. DON'T GIVE ME NONE OF YOUR EXPERIMEN-TAL TREATMENTS, JOHN HOPKINS! She put her foot down on a blood transfusion. YOU AIN'T GONNA GIVE ME AIDS, JOHN HOPKINS! (Actually, she already had AIDS, but maybe she thought I didn't know that.) No matter how she acted, and she did a fair job of simulating demonic possession, the staff just regrouped and strategized. They brought in her long-suffering sons, her social worker, her doctor. They waited two hours and came back. They smothered her with *darling*s and *dear*s. They got her well.

Though my primary view was of the Miss Simpson scenario, I was also riveted by what I could make out of the hospital at large. I watched the troops come and go—the phlebotomists from many lands, the meal carts, the laundry wagons, the night nurses and the day nurses, the white-coated doctors on rounds, their pontifications booming up and down the hall, the flocks of nursing students in navy scrubs, the wheelchairs and gurneys rolling back and forth to radiology, the nutritionists and the visitors. *Can I get an ice water for my dad, please?*

One afternoon I opened my eyes and there were two osteoporotic ladies standing next to my bed with bursting tote bags. Since I'd checked JEWISH as my religion when I was admitted, these representatives had come to bring me grape juice from Israel, challah rolls, and get-well cards from the children of their temple.

"Wow," I said. "This is great. I almost registered as atheist, but maybe now I'll just stay Jewish."

"You should," they told me firmly.

On Friday night, Miss Simpson went home and weekend nurses replaced Geri and Lucky. These were sad farewells, and suddenly, the silence was unearthly. I was the last one on the island. But the truth was, my arm still looked like hell and I was happy to soak up a few more days of rest and nursing.

Checking my e-mail one day, I found an interesting message. It was from a local scientist—a divorced, fifty-year-old father of two, who had been following my biweekly columns in the *Baltimore Fishbowl*. He had ordered and read a couple of my books as well. He went on charmingly about my writing, then said that he'd read in the most recent edition of the column that my search for a boyfriend in Baltimore had been a bust. He proposed that, if the position was still open, he take me out for a cup of coffee.

I hopped right over to Google to see what I could see, and there he was, best-selling science author, Wikipedia entry and all. Though it was hard to type with my arm tethered to the IV pole in a vertical sling, I replied in short order: "Why the hell not." I said I'd let him know when I "got out of hosp."

Before I went home on Sunday, the attending physician brought me some big news. My viral load was down to zero. If I remained undetectable for six months after treatment, I would be considered cured.

The Brainiac came over for tea shortly after I got home from hosp. Prior to our meeting, once I could type with all my fingers, I explained that after a long series of humiliating and idiotic experiences, I had placed a ban on dating and was no longer looking for a boyfriend. Due to the physical and psychological effects of my illness, getting a man was now about as important to me as getting a guinea pig. Yet I was so impressed with the Brainiac's credentials and his generous e-mail that I could not resist meeting him.

I was still fairly etiolated at that point, but over the next few months, I began to regain my strength. The Brainiac took me out to nice restaurants, charmed my friends, took afternoons off from the lab to go to the movies or hiking. At one of our dinners out, I ordered the first glass of wine I'd had in quite some time. It was excellent, and soon I had another. It's not recommended to drink while on the treatment, but I seemed to sneak by. Good blood work, no liver lesions, no problem. Perhaps this is one of the many ways in which I am my mother's daughter. Jane Winik was a stubborn devotee of her pleasures, which she refused to call addictions. She stopped eating three days before she died, but she smoked a cigarette that morning. She was a couple of months away from turning eighty. I hope to follow her model in that regard as well.

As soon as the Brainiac appeared on the scene, people were asking about him. They were excited that I seemed to have a boyfriend. Somehow, though, I did not feel like I had a boyfriend. I wasn't sure if it was a treatment side effect, or a chemistry problem, or him, or me, or just a slow burn.

It's never simple, is it.

the fixer-upper

One thing the Brainiac had going for him was his unblinking acceptance of my health situation. Our first date was essentially a sickbed visit with a cup of tea. I've learned that people have different reactions to scary viruses and serious illness. Some fade into the distance, sending vague e-mails of support, while others step into the breach, hauling your groceries. One friend believed that being exposed to me would pose a slight but fatal risk to her newborn baby. Though this fear had no basis in medical fact, even letters from my doctor could not convince her otherwise. The fatal risk was actually to our friendship.

The relationship that endured the biggest transformation was the one between me and Jane, who underwent a rapid if somewhat forced transition from little girl to independent young woman at the age of eleven. When I first started to be so tired all the time, she was not sympathetic. It was hard for her to accept that I was sick, especially since I had never been sick before. She had been watching me bounce around the house like a silver marble in a pinball machine all her life, and at first she reacted to my slow roll to the drain by being very cranky and critical. Why did I lie on the couch all day and night? Why didn't I cook anymore? Various neighbors had to drive her to and from school, or she walked. In the evenings, we ate take-out lo mein and watched television.

Disturbingly, after the cellulitis episode and the five-day hospitalization were over, I kept going downhill. I was so low-energy I felt like my body was sliding off my bones—like my bones themselves were coming unglued, and I would soon be a formless glob on the couch. One morning after Jane left the house, I broke down and lost it completely. "I can't take it anymore!" I wailed. The dog looked around anxiously, then brought me a tennis ball, hoping a game of fetch might help. Then the phone rang and it was my young doctor. He told me that a follow-up MRI of my arm had shown I might have a life-threatening abscess. I should leave for the hospital immediately.

I literally howled at this news, but he was firm. Soon I had canceled the next day's classes, Crispin was on his way to take care of Jane, and I was back on the eighth floor of Hopkins, this time revealed not to be a spa at all.

I could have nothing to eat or drink the whole time, just in case I ended up in surgery. The nurses were preoccupied with crises elsewhere on the ward. My loud, assertive roommate talked on her cell phone all day, shouting over the gospel DVD she had going on the television.

"Are you one of those people who sleep with the TV on?" she asked me in a break between calls.

"Not really," I said.

"Sorry in advance, then," she said. "I can't sleep without it."

That night, she left the thing tuned to the Patients' Rights Network, which endlessly repeated a ten-minute program advising you what to do with your valuables when you got to the hospital. At about 3:00 a.m., I decided to get up and turn it off. She'd been conked out for hours, and as far as I could see, she didn't even actually wake up, just clicked the remote and turned it back on in her sleep.

The life-threatening abscess was a false alarm, but it was a good thing I'd gone into the hospital, because there was a different, not much less serious problem. My red blood count was about as low as it can go. This is why I felt so horrible. I received two units of blood and was released the next day.

Whoa. The feeling of rejuvenation was incredible. I went running around for at least seventy-two hours, telling everyone I was Keith Richards and blood was the new coke. I walked to Jane's school to pick her up for the first time in a year. I combed my hair and brushed my teeth. I read the whole *Hunger Games* trilogy in a day and a half.

Then it wore off.

Fortunately, around this time, the first three months of treatment came to an end. I got to stop taking Telaprevir and was also put on some shots to boost my red count. Both of these measures improved my well-being considerably, and my arm was slowly returning to normal. Unfortunately, the dryness and itchiness that had started the whole damn thing persisted, and now my eyes, mouth, and nose were all glued together. One day, I got a nosebleed that just wouldn't stop. To explain the stupid way I handled this situation, a little backstory is required.

From the outset, my parents saw me as a fixer-upper, and engaged many contractors to rehab my lazy eye, crooked teeth, pigeon toes, persistent chubbiness, and so on. The prow of the whole pontoon was my nose. It was big, humped at the bridge, and fleshy at the tip. A slightly more refined version of it looks excellent on my twenty-three-year-old son, but my parents were not wrong in thinking that it didn't suit a thirteen-year-old girl. They may have been a little wrong in taking me in for a nose job as a birthday present.

I looked through the book of noses the doctor showed me and knew two things: One, if I did this, I would end up with a miniature pig snout like certain unfortunates in my Hebrew school class; and two, my parents did not love me.

My nose remained proudly untouched for nearly a decade. During this period, I went to college and got a boyfriend named Jan. He was a filmmaker, an ice-hockey player, and an aspiring expatriate. Chameleon girlfriend that I was, I embraced all of these interests. Having had little success in the cinema and as an expat, I tried ice hockey, joining a previously all-male league at the ice rink in Austin, Texas. The entire league was made up of Canadians who had been transferred to Texas by IBM. I didn't even know how to skate when I started, but soon developed my own version of a move called the "submarine check," which basically involved trying to get other players to trip over me.

I was an audience draw, I believe, but it all came screeching to a halt the day I took a slap shot in the face.

This career-ending injury resulted in a whole new conformation for my nose. Now I looked like the bastard child of Barbra Streisand and Wayne Gretzky.

Ever stalwart, I did not seek medical attention until several years later. Ironically enough, I was trying to demonstrate my submarine-check maneuver to a new beau on a sidewalk outside a bar. Caught up in my demonstration, I pretend-skated right into a fire hydrant and mangled my knee.

At the emergency room I was treated by an ex-army doc named Davis. Davis's specialty in the service had been trauma / plastic surgery, and he asked if he might examine my odd-looking nose. The gist of his report was that it was all messed up inside from the accident, and I would have problems in later years—to the point that a rhinoplasty might even be paid for by insurance.

Well, that did it. Up in New Jersey, my mother was horrified that I was having my nose done by a battlefield medic, but to me it was reassuring. She completely embarrassed me by vetting all his licenses and credentials, then flew down for the operation and its aftermath, ready to pass on the wraparound sunglasses she had worn after her eye lift.

When it was over, I had the nose of my dreams—small and cute, but not *too* small and cute, somehow conveying a pleasant memory of whatever had been okay about the original. For thirty years, the finely proportioned nose Dr. Davis gave me has been the cornerstone of my self-esteem.

More recently, however, I have come to feel there might still be something a little weird about the inside of my beautiful nose. Annoying dryness and stuffiness culminated last spring—way before I started hep treatment, like around the time I was first starting to feel weird—in a distressing twenty-four-hour nosebleed. This landed me in the emergency room yet again, where a brutal doctor named Cooramaswamy shoved my head between her giant breasts to muffle my shrieks as she inserted an apparatus through my nostrils into the center of my brain. Various tampon-like appendages and tubes hung down in front to my chin. She told me to go home and come back and see her Monday to have it removed.

I couldn't believe she expected me to walk around all weekend like that, and then, to voluntarily return.

I got home to find the members of a prearranged dinner party waiting for me, so I disguised the lower half of my face with a bandanna and proceeded to serve the boeuf bourguignon as the Frito Bandito on Percodan. Later that evening, alone in my bed, I steeled myself to perform the delicate yet unflinching removal of the unsightly item I have since learned to call a Rapid Rhino 351 Epistaxis Device.

Dr. Cooramaswamy had been unimpressed when I tried to tell her about Dr. Davis's long-ago concerns for my future nose health, and the ENT specialist she referred me to was even less interested in my backstory. From the moment he walked into the room, his ruddy complexion and sculpted hairdo saying "televangelist," I felt uneasy. He took one look up my nose and said disgustedly, "Do you do coke?"

"Well," I said, taken aback, "not for quite a while. Decades, really."

"I can't help you," he told me. "You have a hole in your septum the size of a Buffalo nickel, and your only hope is reconstructive plastic surgery. There's just one man who can do it." He scribbled the name of this superhero on a prescription pad, handed it to me, and left without another word.

I was so humiliated by these incidents, not to mention so weary of dealing with the medical establishment, that when I had a similar nosebleed a few months after my cellulitis episode, I decided to treat it at home no matter what. A week after I'd successfully stopped the nosebleed with my own homemade version of the Rapid Rhino 351 Epistaxis Device, I began to smell something very foul with every breath. Somehow a small wad of Kleenex remained floating around deep in my sinuses, rotting away, and damned if it didn't take a trip to the emergency room—perhaps the most humiliating of all—to have it removed with nasal forceps. I apologized to the doctor for the grossness of the whole procedure. She said, "Yes, but I find it sort of satisfying."

I don't think I did that much coke, really, and even my sister, who tends to have a sharper take on such matters, agrees with me. Nonetheless, the wages of sin and narcissism just keep rolling in. As a greeting card I tacked on my bulletin board years ago says, "If you can't be a good example, you'll just have to serve as a horrible warning."

I really cannot explain why I am so much happier than I was three years ago. It doesn't make sense. I've had no success on the dating front, I've been sick as a dog, and I haven't even lost weight because of it. My twenty-four-year-old son earns more than twice as much as I do. His younger brother makes me look like a wimp in almost every way. My twelve-year-old daughter is prettier and more level-headed. (Come to think of it, perhaps these things are causes of, and not detriments to, my happiness.) In any case, most of my body parts no longer bear any scrutiny whatsoever, which is less critical than it would be if I could actually see them.

The hottest experience I've had in a while was introducing Jane to the DVD of *Shakespeare in Love*. Jane was dubious at first, what with the Elizabethan outfits and the English accents, but once Will and Lady Violet began to gaze into each other's eyes, she couldn't look away.

There are things that happen in life you cannot laugh at. They are few and hopefully far between. These were between years for me, and I'll take as many more of them as I can get.

afterword:
where are they now

Most of the names in this book have been changed and
certain other details adjusted to protect the identities of
the gentlemen involved. While a few are now off my
radar, like Wheelchair Mike and Brown Lips, I've kept
tabs on most of the others, and quite a few have read and
approved their sections of this narrative, as awkward as that
may sound. (I knew that despite my attempts at disguise,
each would recognize himself if he ran into the book, and
other people might, too. So I asked them to read what I
had written and see if they agreed that this was what happened. In most cases, I made any changes they suggested.)

Here's a rundown.

Humberto: About six months after our rendezvous,
the crew was working at another house in my neighborhood. Humberto started coming over at lunchtime, eating at my kitchen table. I didn't mind; in fact, it seemed
sort of sweet to me that he felt we were friends after what

211

went down. We talked about his brother, who had ended up back home in Salvador for now.

After about a week, though, somebody ratted him out, and his boss, who is a friend of mine, came over to find out what was going on. I blanched when I realized how angry he was and how much trouble Humberto might be in. I tried my best to minimize the situation, saying that we were actually friends and he did nothing wrong, and please, please don't fire him. Anything that was out of line was my fault.

The boss gave me a look. Okay, he said, but he has to learn how to behave with clients. You're not helping him if you encourage him to be unprofessional.

About a year later, I wrote down the story, changing some identifying details to confuse the INS in case I published it. Since Humberto couldn't read or speak English, I couldn't get his comments. I doubted he would ever even be aware of its existence, but his boss definitely would. So I had my friend over one day and said I wanted to show him something, but he had to promise he wouldn't take any action based on what he learned by reading it.

I'm not sure he would have stuck to his agreement, but he didn't have to—it turned out he had already let Humberto go for inappropriate behavior with another lady whose house the crew had been working at.

Apparently this woman had received his advances less enthusiastically than I had. And she was not the only one. Meanwhile, in addition to the family I had heard about in his home country, there were apparently also some little Humbertos living in Atlanta.

Oh, well. I guess we already knew I was an idiot.

The Underwear Model Biologist: When reached by e-mail, he agreed to review his chapter. He was basically flattered at his portrayal but suggested I make a couple small changes to further conceal his identity. The most amusing one was changing the long, inscrutable technical title of his cancer research paper to a different long, inscrutable technical title.

Uncle Norm: As of season eleven, he still shows up for an occasional *American Idol* with his take-out Chinese food and his clever little dog, whom we took care of one time when Norm was out of town. He is still dating the yoga teacher he met on Match.com.

Bmoreguy: Remember, he wasn't interested in me "carnally." Sadly, this guy had a second chance to reject me when I relapsed on OkCupid and Plentyoffish about a year after meeting him through Match. He favorited my profile the second I put it up. I couldn't believe it. But when I wrote and reminded him who I was, it turned out that he hadn't recognized (or remembered) me. Sorry, my mistake, he wrote. In reply, I told him I was writing about my experiences and that there was a mention of him—would he like to see it? He demurred. He said he wasn't worried about being "outed," but would prefer not to be in my book, as he "has always been repulsed by authors who manage to profit by telling stories about others' personal lives, or by portraying real people in a less-than-positive light, no matter how disguised they may be; the author still knows their real identity, and it seems like thievery somehow. I think we might have even covered this peccadillo of mine when I mentioned that I had disdain for *The Wire* and for David Simon, for this reason."

Let the repulsion and disdain continue.

Arnie: While a touch concerned about his portrayal in the book, he was most unhappy about the pseudonym Arnie. However, he had no other ideas, and did agree that it was better than using his real name. As former Greenfields campers, Arnie and I have remained friends, and hope to plan another reunion sometime. He called the other day and filled me in on his last few relationships, which turned from potential soul-mate situations to frustrating and confusing disasters. One girl had a brain injury where she couldn't retain visual memories, so she couldn't recognize Arnie, say, when he came out of the bathroom, or from one date to the next. It definitely made for trouble. Another one, with whom he was sure he had a very intense connection, called the cops when a bouquet of flowers he had sent to her arrived on her doorstep. He is a romantic soul, and still very much looking for love. Too bad we didn't click, but in retrospect, we really didn't.

Brett: Still has ridiculous power over me—conceptually, I mean. I haven't seen him again since the Ravens game with the purple coleslaw, but revising the chapter about the kisses was almost as dangerous as experiencing them. His response to reading it was, "Jesus. What a doucher. This guy is a total loser, great kisser or not. I am sorry. Being the private person I am, if you decide to publish this, I would ask that you change enough things to make me unidentifiable. Not only do I value my relative personal anonymity, but I'd also be embarrassed for anyone who knows me to see what an ass I can be." So actually, Joe Fiennes is not the movie star he looks most like. Anyway, I need to stop writing this paragraph before I get sucked into the vortex yet again.

J.J. Johnson: This guy is a prince among men and was very nice about his chapter in the book. He complimented my memory, corrected tiny details of his backstory, and asked if I still had a cute butt.

The Walrus: Jane and I still go see him in his parade every year, and he is always sweet and welcoming. He said it was a very strange experience to read about himself in my manuscript. He had no corrections and said he was mostly flattered, though he did not think it suitable for family and friends.

Zach Silverman: I had to take a deep breath before I showed it to him, because I felt particularly stupid about this incident. Like Brett, he was appalled by his own behavior. He was glad I had explained how drunk he was.

The Pheromone King: We are still in close contact, though every time I talk to him he seems to suggest that he is on his way out of this life very soon. He has been an invaluable source of support and information during this whole hepatitis thing. I hope he gets a liver transplant and outlives us all.

The Brainiac: He thought he came off pretty well. He seemed to like being called the Brainiac.

Crispin: He has firmly stated his intention never to read this book, and I support that decision. Not because I am worried about how I portray him, or our breakup, but because even after all that has happened, it would kill him (or at least make him very ill) to read these stories about me and other men. We remain friends and cordial co-parents. As of this writing, he is still single . . . as far as I know.

At this point, I have accepted the permanence of my tattoo of his initials. I think it's better to live with the evidence of that mad love than to try to cover it up or remove it. Passion leaves marks.

acknowledgments

I would never have written this book without the incredible enthusiasm of Jessica Anya Blau, though I believe she was hoping there would be more sex. Also key were Betsy Boyd and Suzy Dunn, editor and publisher of my column at BaltimoreFishbowl.com, where some of these chapters first appeared. I thank heaven, appearing in the graceful form of Sue Resnick, for sending me Lara Asher of Globe Pequot Press.

There are so many other friends and neighbors and writing buddies and colleagues I am grateful to; I hope you will accept a group hug. If you not only smiled on the writing of this book but were forced to appear in it, I might be able to offer you a Starbucks gift card as well. I must name the person who made every day of these mixed-up years a joy: my daughter, Jane Winik Sartwell.

about the author

Marion Winik is the author of six books of creative nonfiction—*Telling, First Comes Love, The Lunch-Box Chronicles, Rules for the Unruly, Above Us Only Sky,* and *The Glen Rock Book of the Dead*—as well as two volumes of poetry. Her essays and book reviews have appeared in *The New York Times Magazine, The Sun, Salon.com, More, Newsday,* and many other venues. Her commentaries for *All Things Considered* are collected at npr.org. She is a professor at the University of Baltimore. For more information, go to marionwinik.com.